The Narrative Practitioner

Practice Theory in Context series
Series Editor: Jan Fook

Change is rife in welfare organisations but expectations for sound and effective practice continue to rise. More than ever, professionals need to be able to remake ideas and principles for relevance in a range of different circumstances as well as transfer learning from one context to the next.

This new series focuses on approaches to practice that are common and prevalent in health and social care settings. Each book succinctly explains the theoretical principles of its approach and shows exactly how these ideas can be applied skilfully in the pressurised world of day-to-day practice.

Pitched at a level suitable for students on introductory courses, the books are holistic in ethos, also considering organisational and policy contexts, working with colleagues, ethics and values, self-care and professional development. As such, these texts are ideal too as theory refreshers for early and later career practitioners.

Published

Laura Beres
The Narrative Practitioner

Fiona Gardner
Being Critically Reflective

The Narrative Practitioner

Laura Béres

palgrave
macmillan

First published 2014 by
PALGRAVE MACMILLAN

Palgrave Macmillan in the UK is an imprint of Macmillan Publishers Limited, registered in England, company number 785998, of Houndmills, Basingstoke, Hampshire RG21 6XS.

Palgrave Macmillan in the US is a division of St Martin's Press LLC, 175 Fifth Avenue, New York, NY 10010.

Palgrave Macmillan is the global academic imprint of the above companies and has companies and representatives throughout the world.

Palgrave® and Macmillan® are registered trademarks in the United States, the United Kingdom, Europe and other countries

ISBN: 978–1–137–00547–2

This book is printed on paper suitable for recycling and made from fully managed and sustained forest sources. Logging, pulping and manufacturing processes are expected to conform to the environmental regulations of the country of origin.

A catalogue record for this book is available from the British Library.

A catalog record for this book is available from the Library of Congress.

Typeset by Cambrian Typesetters, Camberley, Surrey

Printed in China

Contents

List of Figures

Preface

What this book is, and is not

Narrative practices attempt to move away from totalizing descriptions of people, so I acknowledge that there is a risk of being inconsistent and totalizing myself if I describe myself as a narrative practitioner and a social worker. There is more to me than these two aspects, and yet they influence everything I do. It is also due to the fact that I am *both* a narrative practitioner and a social worker that Jan Fook asked me if I would be interested in writing a book for this series she is editing regarding theories in practice. She told me that she was looking for something other than a typical textbook; she was hoping that the series could be made up of books in which social work practitioners of particular approaches would write more personally about their experiences of actually putting theory into practice. Even textbooks that incorporate case examples and attempt to make the link between theory and practice do not always reflect on the challenges of continuing to practise within a particular framework once a person is working in an agency or organizational setting. Theories, as they are explained in textbooks, can run the risk of seeming too straightforward or too 'pure' in their descriptions to inspire belief in their practicality once a student has graduated and is in what might be called the 'real world'. Therefore, at Jan's prompting, what I have attempted in this book is to describe what I have found to be the most inspiring and useful aspects of narrative practice, to reflect on the challenges I have experienced and witnessed in students as they have begun the process of learning narrative skills for ongoing practice, and to fill in some gaps in the literature in terms of how narrative therapy might address issues of agency-based practice, research, spirituality and even self-care.

Potentially unsettling new areas

There are certain discourses that are called on by the terms 'agency-based practice', 'research', 'spirituality' and 'self-care' that might be offputting for

some practitioners who are already committed to the politics and philosophical underpinnings of narrative therapy. When I was first learning and
incorporating narrative ways of working into my practice, I might also have
been quite concerned by what I am now attempting to do in this book.
Although there are ways of taking up all these topics that could reinforce
traditional, mainstream ways of thinking about practice and the structure of
society, I have attempted to consider these topics within the framework of
the philosophy and politics of narrative therapy in order to think through
how narrative practitioners may be able to deal with these issues that their
colleagues raise quite regularly. I think the fact that I am attempting to deal
with these topics might be a relief for some narrative practitioners and
might frustrate others.

The Dulwich Centre has recently announced that it has developed a part-
nership with the Department of Social Work at the University of Melbourne
in Australia and will be offering a joint Master of Narrative Therapy and
Community Work degree commencing in March 2014 (www.dulwichcen-
tre.com.au). In Chapter 1 I describe the way in which White and
Denborough (2005) have discussed the care and thought that have gone into
the development of publishing and training events offered by the Dulwich
Centre. This care is also being taken in deciding the forms of research to
integrate into the Master's programme that will be congruent with the politics, values and philosophy of narrative therapy. Narrative practice will
continue to evolve and develop as it continues to address the concerns of
people and communities who request services, and also as it reflects on how
to integrate research and the needs of practitioners working in a variety of
contexts. I also reflect on some of these challenges in Chapter 6, regarding
inquiry and critical reflection of practice.

I received my training in narrative practice from Michael White (2006,
2007b), Shona Russell and others (2006) in Australia through programmes
offered by the Dulwich Centre and from both Michael White (1995b, 2005)
and David Epston (2009, 2012) in workshops they have facilitated in
Canada and the United States. I have also had the privilege of learning from
Michael White by working alongside him in a community practice project
in south-western Ontario (www.neighbouringcommunities.net). Although
some trainers of narrative therapy and some students when they are first
learning the practice skills may be concerned about 'doing it right' as if it
were a static set of skills that can be learnt and honed and polished to
perfection, what has been inspiring to me about both Michael White and
David Epston has been what I have interpreted as their love of learning and
their commitment to not being hemmed in by expectations of theories. In
learning narrative practice skills, there is the risk of wanting to model
ourselves on White and Epston as the originators of narrative therapy,

which can mean trying to duplicate what we have seen them do and then inadvertently reifying the practice as they first developed it. If we truly are to model ourselves on them, this would also mean voraciously reading a wide range of literature from a broad range of disciplines and constantly reflecting on how we might further improve our practice, responding always to changing social pressures and new learning. I have heard White use Geertz's term 'copying that originates' (White, 2006) at the end of training conferences to encourage trainees not to worry about trying to be exactly the same as the trainers of narrative practice. He would encourage us to accept the fact that even if we attempted to 'copy', we would in fact be developing our own original ways of practising. I have presented in this book some of the basic conversation maps that White developed and have at the same time taken seriously his encouragement to originate ideas as well, moving into areas that narrative therapists and trainers have not previously explored.

Narrative therapy is very much influenced and shaped by post-modern and post-structuralist theory. My approach to writing this book has also been very much influenced by these theories, and although I draw on research articles and traditional sources that would usually be quoted in academic texts, I have also been influenced by personal communications and internet sources, so I give them credit and reference these also. Although this has not been the norm in formal academic texts, where high-quality peer-reviewed journals would be valued more than personal conversation, this does, in fact, represent the reality of how ideas in general, and a post-modern approach to therapeutic practice in particular, evolve.

In discussing the underlying philosophy of narrative therapy in more detail in Chapter 1, I describe why I write personally using 'I' rather than attempting to make myself sound more objective by using a neutral academic voice. I also point out a commitment within narrative writing to move away from the language of 'client'. As I have already suggested, the discourses called on by certain words may inadvertently reinforce mainstream hierarchical relationships. I have attempted, instead, to describe conversations with 'people' and to use phrases and words that do not rely on traditional therapeutic and helping discourses. Despite this attempt, because I am also referring to a wide range of literature and not only drawing on the literature written by narrative practitioners, there will be some slippage in the use of these terms as I quote from others and refer to their work. My hope is that readers will keep in mind the fact that I am stressing the politics and philosophy of narrative therapy first and foremost in Chapter 1, and that this should be read as needing to influence everything else that follows. As Furlong (2008) points out, White was not convinced that narrative therapy should be reduced to the status of an approach, but rather should be considered a worldview, 'an epistemology, a philosophy, a personal commitment, a politics, a practice, a life' (White in Furlong, 2008, p. 404).

A little bit of backdrop

Narrative practices are of interest to a range of counsellors, psychologists, therapists, social workers and community organizers, and this book has developed in such a way that it will be of interest to a range of practitioners. Initially, however, considering this series to be geared towards a UK social work audience, I met with some social work academics in England in the summer of 2012. I was particularly interested in hearing from them about whether they thought social workers in the United Kingdom would be interested in a book about narrative therapy. I was warned that most social workers in the United Kingdom do not believe that they have time to do 'therapy' and so might, therefore, not be overly interested initially in narrative therapy. Funnily enough, Furlong (2008) and Epston (in personal communication) have reminded me that Michael White and David Epston were both social workers; narrative therapy is one of the few approaches within social work that has been developed by social workers and is applicable to social workers. Nonetheless, what was pointed out to me at the same time was that a great many social workers in the United Kingdom work in child protection and that the recent Munro Review of Child Protection (Munro, 2011) might provide a useful context in which to ground a discussion of narrative practice and its possibilities for child protection work.

The Munro Review has presented a series of recommendations that Munro believes will 'help to reform the child protection system from being over-bureaucratized and concerned with compliance to one that keeps a focus on children' (Munro, 2011, p. 8). The report is extensive and thorough, reviewing the driving forces that have shaped the current protection system in England and then, based on interviews with families and children who have received services as well as front-line protection workers and managers, presents eight principles that underpin the review's recommendations. These principles are as follows:

1. The system should be child centred.
2. The family is usually the best place for bringing up children and young people.
3. Helping children and families involves working *with* them and therefore the quality of the relationship between the child and family and professionals has direct impacts on the effectiveness of help given.
4. Early help is better for children.

5. Children's needs and circumstances are varied, so the system needs to offer equal variety in its responses.
6. Good professional practice is informed by knowledge of the latest theory and research.
7. Uncertainty and risk are features of child protection work; risk management can only reduce risks, not eliminate them.
8. The measure of the success of child protection systems, both local and national, is whether children are receiving effective help. (Munro, 2011, p. 26)

I am convinced that the underlying philosophy of narrative therapy and the actual practice skills that I describe in this book will assist people in developing practices that are consistent with the recommendations Munro has presented in her review. In particular, I will provide methods to respond to her comments about the importance of relationships that foster a commitment to working *with* people, privileging the hopes of each unique family, and reflection of practice as an approach to developing practice-based evidence and professional confidence.

Acknowledgements

As is clear from my comments in the Preface, this book would not have come about without Jan Fook's interest, and for this I thank her. Jan introduced me to Catherine Gray of Palgrave Macmillan and the process of writing this book began. I thank both Jan and Catherine for their ongoing commitment to this project, their encouragement and their wise counsel.

Hugh Fox, of the Institute of Narrative Practices in the United Kingdom, and his colleague Mark Hayward have indicated in personal email communication that they believe narrative practices are currently primarily used in the United Kingdom by clinical psychologists in the National Health Service and educational psychologists in local authorities. Hugh indicated, however, that he started his career as a social worker and believes that social workers would be very interested in and able to integrate narrative practices into their work. Liz Todd of Newcastle University teaches narrative practices and (also in personal email communication) suggested that in her experience a wide range of professional practitioners in the United Kingdom are interested in working from a narrative practice perspective. This has contributed to my hope that this book will be of interest to a range of practitioners in various settings in the United Kingdom. I thank Hugh, Mark and Liz for sharing their thoughts and encouragement.

I appreciate David Epston's support and encouragement over the past several years. He is an inspiring role model who is committed to the constant development of ideas and practice skills. I am particularly grateful for his interest in this writing project and his suggestion that I visit Walter Bera and talk with him about how he has integrated narrative practice ideas into all aspects of administration and provision of service at the Kenwood Therapy Center. I am grateful to Walter for his hospitality and generosity in sharing forms and procedures that have enriched this book with concrete examples. I also thank David for encouraging me to speak directly about the contributions that Michael White made to my practice and how his legacy continues to influence and inspire the narrative practice and social work worlds.

Although this book developed since Michael's death and so he has not had a direct influence on its focus, the fact that I was able to train with him and work alongside him in a community project will continue to have ongoing effects in my practices. Even when I am not directly quoting Michael's work, his influence on my philosophy and politics of therapy cannot help but be present and implicit. I will always be immensely grateful to Michael for his friendship, and his interest in, and support of, my work. As he discussed in his interview with Duvall and Young (2009, p. 14), there is an element of 'keeping faith' in the values and principles at the centre of his work that he role modeled and that will continue to inspire me and, of course, many others.

I also wish to mention Cheryl White's influence. She was the first person I met at the Dulwich Centre when I began my training there. Her presence and her commitment to the underlying commitments of narrative therapy in all that she does at the Dulwich Centre made for a particularly welcoming, enriching and supportive environment for learning new skills. I remember mentioning to Michael that although I had attended some of his workshops in Canada, there was something quite different and wonderful about learning narrative practices at the Dulwich Centre. He agreed there was something special there and I am sure that Cheryl contributed significantly to that difference. I am grateful for her interest in my work, for staying in touch over the years, and particularly for the permission she provided to allow me to use figures of conversation maps for which the Dulwich Centre holds copyright. The originals can be found on the Dulwich Centre website (www.dulwichcentre.com.au) in Michael White's workshop notes, which are posted in the Articles to Read section.

I am also grateful to Joanna Bedggood, Coralee Berlemont, Hiedi Britton-deJeu, Sandy Ferreira, Diane Gingrich and Melissa Page Nichols, who all contributed case studies or notes on self-care, which have enriched this book by grounding the ideas in a wider range of practice settings than I would have been able to do by myself.

As ever, I am grateful to my husband, David, for putting up with how distracted I can be while writing, and for being interested in and supportive of this project and the ideas inherent in narrative practice. I appreciate being able to discuss my descriptions of this way of working with him, since his feedback on whether or not I am being clear is invaluable. Finally, I would like to thank my son, Liam, who was also kind enough to show an interest in my writing and gently remind me to check on the proper use of commas, colons and semi-colons, so as not to horrify reviewers of the first draft of the manuscript.

The authors and publisher would like to thank the following individuals and organizations for permission to reproduce copyright material:

The Dulwich Centre for permission to reproduce the 'Re-authoring conversation map', the 'Externalizing conversation (statement of position map 1), the 'Externalizing conversation map (statement of position map 2)', the 'Remembering conversation map', the 'Re-authoring conversation map' and the' Outside witnessing conversation map', adapted from White, *Maps of Narrative Practice* (2007) and Russell et al, *Seven Month Narrative Therapy Training Programme* (2006).

Walter Bera for his permission to reproduce Appendix 1, Appendix 2 and Appendix 3 in this book from Bera, *Practicing Narrative Therapy in Modernist Settings: Innovative Approaches to Assessment, Diagnosis, Treatment Charting and More* (2013), for Appendix 4 in this book, from the Kenwood Therapy Center (2013) and for Appendix 5 in this book, from Bera, *Narragrams: Visualizing Narrative Therapy 2e* (2013). Written permission for use or adaptation of these forms can be obtained by emailing Walter Bera at w.bera@kenwoodcenter.org.

PART

I

The Narrative Approach

1 An Introduction to Narrative Practice

Introduction

I was recently at a social event where a woman seated beside me at dinner asked me what I do. I told her I am a social worker. She asked me a little more, so I explained I am particularly interested in teaching, researching and writing in the area of narrative practice. She then heaved a great sigh and asked me when society's obsession with narratives had begun. She said that she is constantly hearing people talk about narratives and about being interested in knowing other people's stories and that she is fed up with it. She appeared to think it all a little ridiculous, as she went on to say she had read lots of novels as a child and so she understood stories to be made up and untrue. As I was dithering about whether to respond to these comments within this setting, the other three women at the table, all of them in different fields, started to describe the way in which they believed stories add richness to our understanding of life. The historian, for instance, said that two different accounts of events in history could have all the same facts included, but the one that presented the events with a greater appreciation of the details of narrative would be far more engaging of people's interest.

Not only does the word 'narrative' crop up more often in the media and popular culture now than it did even ten years ago, there has also been a great deal written about the use of narratives within counselling and social work, and in the growing area of narrative medicine (Charon, 2006). Different disciplines and approaches to practice draw on the use of stories, or narratives, in different ways, however.

When I describe narrative therapy, I am describing the underlying philosophy, stance and practice skills as they have been developed by White and Epston (1990), rather than describing a general process of engaging people in telling their stories or using narratives in therapy. I will use both the terms 'narrative therapy' and 'narrative practice', since much of the earlier literature has focused on narrative therapy as a distinct form of direct micro-level practice, but the underlying theory and skills are applicable to community practice and agency-based social services, so the term narrative practice has begun to be used more often as it is more descriptive of the broad range of practice possibilities within this framework. This shift in terms also speaks to some of the underlying commitments within narrative practice, which I will discuss in detail throughout this book, and which have to do with moving away from mainstream therapeutic discourses and medical models.

Although I grew up in England and received the majority of my training in narrative therapy in Australia, I now teach narrative practices and social work in a Canadian university, maintaining a small independent consulting and counselling practice. Social work in Canada involves the same types of practice as social work in the United Kingdom, including case management in local authorities, child protection agencies and hospitals; with interdisciplinary health teams; social welfare policy analysis; community organizing and development; and advocacy. It also includes opportunities for school-based practice and clinical social work, focusing on counselling and psychotherapy with small groups, individuals, couples and families, which is not as usual for social workers in the United Kingdom. My descriptions and examples of narrative practice will, therefore, be applicable to social workers, child protection workers, counsellors and therapists, as well as doctors and nurse practitioners engaged in counselling and direct practice.

Although narrative ways of working lend themselves to community practice, and despite the fact I have been able to work alongside Michael White in a community project in south-western Ontario, I will not describe narrative community work in this book. This is partly because my experiences with this project are specific to a North American context where land rights for Indigenous communities continue to require well-thought-out responses.[1] It is also because others with far more experience with community practice have written extensively about narrative work in a variety of community settings.[2]

I am committed to teaching, researching and writing about narrative practices within a transnational context because I believe that the underlying philosophy and politics of narrative practices are consistent with the social justice and anti-oppressive frameworks of the profession of social work and engage respectfully with various cultures and within various local contexts. I also believe that narrative practices provide an approach that respects the strengths and preferences of those people who request counselling, while at the same time acknowledging the pain and difficulties that have contributed to the development of their resilience. Although it may be considered a strengths-based approach to practice, it is not only solution focused and plenty of time is given to understanding and deconstructing the problem.

I have organized this book in two parts. In the first part I review the underlying theory, philosophy and ethics of narrative practice and the conversation maps as White developed them. I will also include a chapter regarding what is often absent (not explicit), but rather implicit in conversations, and the steps involved in such conversations to assist people in reconnecting to their knowledge, skills and preferred ways of living. I will conclude the first half of the book with a short chapter regarding a proposed meta map to aid in the process of thinking through when to use particular conversation maps and when to consider moving from one map to another. This meta map primarily came about in response to requests from students for further clarity about how to visualize the maps coming together.

The second part of the book is about practising within a narrative framework in agency and organizational contexts, and the challenges associated with attempting to maintain a commitment to narrative practices despite all the demands that arise in the real world of practice. In the first of these chapters I will reflect on working with colleagues and teams and finding ways to complete all the paperwork associated with professional practice from a narrative perspective. In the following chapters I will discuss the benefits of integrating critical reflection of practice as a form of ongoing inquiry and accountability, issues related to integrating a respect for spirituality in practice and finally, thoughts on self-care.

I will follow the same practice as that developed by Michael White and David Epston (1990) and also followed by Martin Payne (2006), whereby I will describe people who come to counselling or use social work services as 'people' rather than 'clients', 'patients' or 'service users'. I will use the terms 'social worker', 'counsellor' and 'therapist', since narrative practices can be used within all the professions suggested by these terms. I also allow my own voice and opinions to be clear through the use of 'I', which is consistent with the philosophical and political underpinnings of narrative practices. One of the most important aspects of narrative therapy is its commitment to moving away from discourses that privilege the professional's objectivity and knowledge over the skills, knowledge and expertise of those people who request the services of professionals (Epston, 2009; White, 1995a). Although narrative practitioners develop expertise in the practice skills associated with narrative therapy, it is important to recognize they can never know as much about someone's life as the person who has actually lived that life. Within narrative therapy there is a commitment to socially just practice that necessarily involves reflecting on structures of power and the resulting interactions that can reinforce unjust relationships (White, 1995a, 2007a).

The beginnings of narrative therapy

The website of the Dulwich Centre, in Adelaide, South Australia, provides a wealth of information regarding the development of narrative therapy, connections to narrative practitioners around the world, many links to articles and information about ongoing projects. The website indicates that the centre was first opened in 1983 and has continued to develop since then:

> First, a way of working, 'narrative approaches to counselling and community work' has evolved, particularly inspired by the work of Michael White and David Epston. This way of working has now moved from being a marginal approach to one that is now considered a mainstream modality in many contexts. Second, a 'community of ideas' and a 'community of practitioners' has grown in different parts of the world. This community is linked in many ways – through ideas and practices, through the written word (journals and books), through Narrative Connections and other websites and e-lists, and through workshops and conferences. So many people have contributed to these developments in different ways. (www.dulwichcentre.com.au/about-dulwich)

Although there are now many narrative therapy and training centres around the world, the Dulwich Centre, of which Michael White was co-director with Cheryl White, is probably most often thought of as the primary centre for learning narrative therapy and community work skills.

David Epston, the co-originator of narrative therapy with Michael White, is co-director, with Johnella Bird, of The Family Therapy Centre, which opened in Auckland, New Zealand in 1988. He also teaches at the School of Community Development, Unitec Institute of Technology, also in Auckland. He travels extensively providing training for beginners and advanced practitioners of narrative therapy.

White has indicated that he and Epston first met at an Australian Family Therapy conference in 1981, where they recognized a 'certain correspondence in [their] respective ideas and practices' (White & Epston, 1990, p. xv), which he suggests was the starting point of their friendship and professional association. Their first book regarding narrative ways of working was initially published by Dulwich Centre Publications in 1989 entitled *Literary Means to Therapeutic Ends*, and then re-published as *Narrative Means to Therapeutic Ends* by W.W. Norton in 1990. Michael White was co-director with Cheryl White of the Dulwich Centre until January 2008, when he set up a new centre, Adelaide Narrative Therapy Centre, with Maggie Carey, Shona Russell and Rob Hall. Following Michael White's death in April 2008, Carey, Russell and Hall developed an independent centre, Narrative Practices Adelaide, which they indicate has been influenced by White's hopes for the ongoing development of collaborative work between various narrative therapy centres (www.narrativepractices.com.au).

In 2005, Cheryl White and David Denborough wrote *A Community of Ideas: Behind the Scenes.* They describe how Cheryl founded Dulwich Centre Publications in 1984 and how feminist thinking has informed the practices of the centre from the beginning. What I particularly appreciate about the book is the detail they provide on the thought, care and step-by-step decision-making process and planning for their work in 'developing training courses that are congruent with narrative ideas' (White & Denborough, 2005, p. 101). They describe taking into account the community context of each conference event, making sure that there is appropriate community involvement each time. For instance, it was important to them to include the Senior Elder of the Kaurna people of the Adelaide Plains in the opening ceremony of their inaugural conference in order to welcome conference participants to the land (p. 51). On the other hand, they describe the welcoming ceremony of their fifth conference, in the multicultural context of Liverpool, United Kingdom, as involving many voices: 'Representatives of the Liverpool Black Community, the Jewish Community, the Chinese Community, the Muslim Community, those of Irish descent, and the Welsh, each welcomed us to their city and linked us to the history of their people' (p. 58).

White and Denborough also describe the commitment within their conferences to ensure space for people who might otherwise feel marginalized by traditional types of conferences. They say, 'these events commonly include a women's gathering; a lesbian or queer welcoming dinner; a lunch or dinner for Indigenous people and/or people of colour; and at times Jewish and Muslim events' (White & Denborough, 2005, p. 48). They describe the manner in which they have developed ways of working in publication and in conference planning that are 'congruent with narrative ideas' (p. 101). This idea that once we are immersed within the politics, philosophy and commitments of narrative practice we are able to think through how other practices besides therapy can also be developed that are congruent with these commitments is important to me. I would argue that this also implies that we are able to examine other practices for their underlying politics, philosophy and commitments in order to reflect on whether these other approaches are congruent with those within narrative therapy. This is why I spend time in Chapter 6 examining which forms of research and inquiry might be congruent with narrative practices.

Finally, it is interesting to note that White and Denborough (2005) also comment on the need for participants of conferences to reflect on their self-care. They describe how they present this idea in a participant handbook in which they say, 'We would like to invite participants into practices of self-care …, and also to invite participants to take care of one another' (p. 119). They go on to encourage people to take a morning or afternoon off if necessary and make sure to get enough sleep. Since I reflect, in Chapter 8, on issues of self-care, which have not usually been discussed by narrative practitioners, I was pleased to rediscover the fact that White and Denborough have also considered these issues in relation to their planning of conferences and training sessions.

Underlying philosophy of narrative therapy[3]

Although I found it helpful to approach narrative therapy in a Dulwich Centre training programme by learning the frameworks of the conversation maps that Michael White developed, some people become frustrated with the maps. White (2007a) describes them as signposts that are only meant to be helpful for providing some structure to narrative conversations and, as such, they are not intended to be rigid or prescriptive.[4] Nevertheless, when first learning narrative practice skills some people seem to get caught up in attempting to practise the conversation maps in some sort of pure manner and then become annoyed, believing that the maps are rigid. I will present the conversation maps because they are extremely helpful when first learning narrative therapy skills, but what I want to stress is that they are more like methods for learning and practising initially: like practising playing scales when learning to play the piano (Russell et al., 2006). The underlying philosophy and politics of narrative therapy are what make narrative practices different from other approaches. Some people might attempt to take up some of the practice skills and techniques of narrative therapy, like externalizing a problem and moving through the steps of an externalizing conversation, but then the skills will only be part of a bag of tricks that might be incorporated into other theoretical frameworks and philosophies. If the philosophy and political stance of narrative therapy are taken up, the practitioner is much more likely to practise as a narrative therapist/social worker even if he or she does not seem always to use the conversation maps. In other words, there is the learning of narrative therapy skills and then there is the taking up of the philosophical stance of narrative therapy; I believe that it is most important for people first of all to decide whether the philosophy of narrative therapy is consistent with their preferences for their practice. This does not necessarily require a return to the primary sources of inspiration for White and Epston, but rather reflection on their use and application of ideas, which previously could have seemed disconnected from direct practice.[5]

Professional posture (relationship)

White (1995a) discusses the professional posture and politics of therapy when he says that he is not suggesting that therapists develop a one-down position, which he believes would be 'ingenuine, patronising, and disquali-fying' (p. 57), but rather that the following is important:

> We can make it our business to structure the context of therapy so that it is less likely to reproduce dominant cultural forms of organization, including those that perpetuate hierarchies of knowledge, and other oppressive practice. And I think that whatever a 'good' therapy is, it will concern itself with establishing structures that will expose the real and potential abuses of power in the practices of the good therapy itself. (White, 1995a, p. 47)

Payne (2006) also suggests that narrative practitioners recognize that ther-apy itself can be potentially harmful when based on unrecognized power relations. He says that narrative practitioners attempt to limit the potential harm by an ongoing examination of their practice and by asking people regularly if they are finding the services they are receiving to be acceptable. He suggests that this is a method by which therapists are able to de-center themselves.

Duvall and I (2011) have previously described the process of critically reflecting on a particular training programme in narrative therapy and our observations of how difficult it was for many trainee therapists to come to terms with what this de-centered therapeutic posture would look like. I see students in the graduate programme where I teach also struggling with what this might mean in practice. What is important for narrative therapists to remember is that a neutral stance will reinforce mainstream cultural and professional discourses. It is not productive merely to abdicate all power in the role of professional practitioner, because this can result in merely listen-ing to the stories of the people who request services, which can inadvertently reinforce the cultural discourses that have contributed to people's problems; however, it is suggested that it is possible to be de-centered and influential at the same time (Russell et al., 2006; White, 1995a, 2005). This means constantly reflecting on the power dynamics in relationships, taking respon-sibility for the therapeutic process and asking the types of questions that are part of the conversation maps White has proposed (2007a). These questions and conversation maps assist people in reflecting on taken-for-granted discourses and cultural expectations that may have limited their options, and support them in reconnecting to their own personal preferences and values for life.

When first learning the questions and structures of the conversation maps, many therapists and social workers can find the phrasing and language awkward and unfamiliar. I believe this is because these questions do unsettle the power dynamics and force practitioners to take responsibility for the effects of the therapeutic posture and professional language they use. Students say that in struggling with trying to learn the language, structure and posture associated with narrative practices, they begin to have trouble being truly present to, and focused on, the people consulting them. This is part of the learning process, as they give up previously familiar ways of being with people and learn to take up the de-centered but influential stance. I reassure them, as I was reassured, that it merely takes practice. The approach does become more comfortable and they will be able to re-experience the feeling of being truly present to the other person in the conversation. The process of learning and practising a new set of skills is like working as an apprentice, as Epston has described it (2009, 2012), and as an apprentice narrative therapist it is useful to spend time watching and practising with more experienced narrative therapists whenever possible.

Ethics and values: as an anti-oppressive practice

In describing the professional posture associated with narrative practice, I have implied a set of ethics and values that underpin this approach, but it is useful to be explicit about these. White (1995a) clarifies, for instance, that when he speaks about values he is referring to 'small "v" values – not those that propose, or are based on, some universal notion of the good, and not those that establish some normalising judgment of persons' (White, 1995a, p. 58). He says that when speaking of values he is, rather, referring to an ethical position. For instance, earlier in that same chapter, he discusses the need for each of us to acknowledge the significance of our own race and ethnic location in the world.

In his descriptions of working ethically with marginalized populations, White (1995a) touches on his work with Aboriginal health services in Australia developing culturally appropriate counselling services for urban Aboriginal people. He did this by working with Aboriginal consultants, rather than by proposing certain approaches from a position of expertise. I would hope that this would seem like common sense now and I am reassured when I see more social workers ensuring that they are not merely recreating mainstream dominant services with marginalized populations or in other countries where they are asked to consult, but this has not always been the tradition within social work.

I am also currently working with a group of Indigenous and non-Indigenous colleagues developing a collaborative research team examining the effects of a pen-pal project between Indigenous and non-Indigenous elementary school children in south-western Ontario in Canada. It has been a fascinating process working together to ensure ethical relationships and reciprocity among ourselves and with potential participants of the research.[6] The process of going through research ethics approval at the university, however, was extremely challenging and frustrating, because we were not fitting into mainstream traditional expectations regarding research. A commitment to working within an anti-oppressive framework and being willing to privilege the ethics of relationship has meant some-times having to stand up against some mainstream expectations regarding traditional research ethics, which can be experienced as colonizing and oppressive to those people outside of the 'mainstream'.

When I describe ethics and notions associated with ethical relationships, it is important also to point out that I am describing something that is not necessarily captured by codes of ethics of professional colleges and associa-tions (e.g., the various provincial Associations of Social Workers and Social Service Workers, and Colleges of Certified Social Workers and Social Service Workers in Canada; or the British Association for Social Workers and General Social Care Councils in the United Kingdom). Codes of ethics from associations often suggest what we should *not* do, rather than what we should do in order to engage ethically and compassionately with others.

Irving (2006), Mullaly (2006) and Rossiter (2006) were all invited to contribute articles for a forum regarding the 2005 Canadian Association of Social Work code of ethics. Each of them had concerns with codes of ethics, for various reasons, but what they had in common was their belief that codes of ethics do not necessarily ensure ethical interactions between people. Codes of ethics from professional organizations are more likely to provide guidelines to limit the legal risk for professionals rather than to provide professionals with encouragement in regard to acting ethically.

Mullaly (2006) worries that the most recent Canadian code of ethics p social workers in the position of juggling the needs of the people we se with the needs of the agencies in which we work, rather than suggesting that the people who come for services should be our primary focus. This is consistent with what Munro (2011) has described as having contributed to the over-bureaucratization and over-concern with compliance in child protection services in England. Rossiter (2006) draws on the work of Emmanuel Levinas in describing the need to take up a not-knowing stance in order to engage ethically with others; and, of course, this is not suggested through codes of ethics. Finally, Irving presents the most radical position, drawing on Foucault, Deleuze, Becket and Bacon, as he remarks: 'my argu-ment, however frail and improbable, is that ethics can only emerge, and then only obliquely, when we view being as not syntactical (Beckett's claim) and consider human and social existence through the lens of intensities (as does Deleuze)' (Irving, 2006, p. 132). He tells us that 'Foucault beseeches us to pull away from old categories and codes that are binding and restrictive and instead to "prefer what is positive and multiple: difference over uniformity, flows over unities, mobile arrangements over systems." Believe that what is productive is not sedentary but nomadic' (pp. 132–3).

The concerns raised by Mullay, Rossiter and Irving, and their suggestions for how to respond to those concerns, are all consistent with the narrative posture and approach to ethics and values. Narrative practitioners are committed to critically reflecting on power and engaging in anti-oppressive practices. We are also committed to privileging the expertise of those people consulting us, and taking up that not-knowing stance as we engage in ethical relationships with them. Finally, narrative therapy is also strongly influenced by post-modern and post-structural thought, from Foucault and Derrida, and so recognizes the fluidity and social construction of identity and stories, and opens up space for people to move towards their preferred ways of being, rather than having to conform to pre-conceived expectations (White, 2007a).

I understand that there is also a great interest in the United Kingdom regarding ethical and appropriate professional relationships across culture and race. However, Gilbert (2009) provides an interesting comparison of the International Federation of Social Workers and the International Association of Schools of Social Workers' statement of principles with the British Association of Social Workers' code of ethics. He raises concerns, similar to those raised by Mullaly, Rossiter and Irving, pointing out that social work is 'promoting a position of providing the illusion of inclusion while excluding many of the most vulnerable, particularly those who do not share Western liberal beliefs or Christian traditions' (Gilbert, 2009, p. 7). He also worries that the state control of agencies providing social care and social work have limited the ability of social workers to engage in anti-oppressive practice, despite the commitments made by codes of ethics to social justice and anti-oppressive practice. These are concerns that should be kept in mind when considering the ideas presented in the second part of this book. There is a tension inherent in working within government-funded agencies when we acknowledge the social structures that continue to marginalize and oppress many of the most vulnerable people with whom we will work. However, most social workers and practitioners will pursue work in agency contexts and so it is useful to think through how best to be able to bring narrative practice commitments and postures to bear on work in these settings. Drawing on Hugman, Gilbert (2009) goes on to suggest that we take up an ethics of care, 'which take caring relationships as the start point; "ethics of compassion" where intelligent use of emotion provides the fulcrum for ethical decision making; an "ethics of life" that takes sustainability as criteria, and post-modern ethics that focus on the contingent, uncertain, and transient nature of contemporary social relationships' (p. 7). The underlying philosophy and politics of narrative therapy are consistent with these ideas about an ethics of care, and the skills associated with narrative therapy provide an approach for putting an ethics of care into practice.

The philosophy and politics, the commitments and the overall stance inherent in narrative practices provide the ethical grounding and anti-oppressive stance for the use of narratives. This is why I have spent this amount of space and time describing them before turning to ideas regarding story structure and the re-authoring of stories within narrative practices.

Elements of story

An engaging account of events, over time, according to a plot or theme

People often ask me when they first hear of my interest in narrative therapy whether narrative therapy is about having people recount their story. Sometimes they ask if it is about reading people stories. All therapies engage people in telling their stories, so there is also some confusion about how narrative therapy might be different from other therapies, if that is the case.

Narrative therapy is different from other approaches to therapy that also have people tell their stories, because of the underlying philosophies, and also because of the explicit understanding of the elements that make up a narrative. It is also different because of the explicit recognition of the social construction of a person's identity through the telling of stories of self and other, and because of the recognition of the possibility of multiple storylines being present in anyone's life.

I sometimes wish that narrative therapy was named something different, because there is this confusion about the use of narratives. It is interesting to reflect that White and Epston's first version of *Narrative Means to Therapeutic Ends* (1990) was in fact entitled *Literary Means to Therapeutic Ends* and I wonder whether 'literary therapy' would have been any less confusing; probably not, although in their early work White and Epston use the analogy of 'text' (White and Epston, 1990, p. 9), arguing that by embracing the text analogy it is possible to understand how in order to 'make sense of our lives and to express ourselves, experiences must be "storied" and it is this storying that determines the meaning ascribed to experience' (p. 10).

In order for people's stories to make sense, the storylines need to be made up of a series of 'events linked in sequence across time in such a way as to arrive at a coherent account of themselves and the world around them' (White and Epston, 1990, p. 10). These stories that are told can be described as having a particular plot or theme that holds the events together into that coherent account. White (2005) has explained that in imagining a good book or movie that has been enjoyed, it is possible to describe the story contained within that book or movie by describing the events of the story. It is possible to describe how the events followed from one to another across time with an understanding of what the plot was of that story. For instance, romance and mystery plots follow particular structures and we can recognize and label them as such.

Narrative therapists recognize that a person's life is made up of innumerable events, many of which do not necessarily seem of importance to that person and so are not told to anyone. Those events that go un-storied are often forgotten and their significance diminishes further; as White (2007a) puts it, 'the myriad experiences of daily life mostly pass like a blip across the screen of our consciousness and into a historical vacuum' (p. 219). When someone requests counselling, or is mandated for home visits due to concerns about child safety, the person will usually present a problem storyline. After all, if there were not problems in the person's life, there probably would not be any need for engagement in services with a social worker or narrative practitioner. If someone recounts a history of having been sexually abused as a child and then having experienced teen dating violence and now struggling with a relationship in which there are ongoing control issues, the problem storyline could be said to have a plot or theme of 'abuse or victimhood'. If a practitioner was only to elicit further descriptions of the problem storyline, the story of abuse would become more entrenched and would be further 'thickened', to use Geertz's term (Geertz, 1973). What a narrative therapist attempts to do is to ask the sort of questions, often through the structure of particular conversation maps, that help the person remember and recount events that have happened in his or her life that have had less attention paid to them previously, but that could be strung together in a preferred plot or storyline. There will also be events in the person's life that do not have to do with being abused, that may be about resisting and standing up to abuse, or even about other behaviours that have nothing to do with abuse at all. These alternative storylines, when people begin to develop them, may seem very weak, or 'thin' (as opposed to Geertz's 'thick' descriptions). These thin storylines are initially vulnerable to being forgotten or minimized, because they have not been socially constructed and shared often enough with others; 'it is the therapist's task to assist people to render significant some of the neglected aspects of lived experience' (White, 2007a, p. 219). The more these new preferred storylines are shared, the thicker and more robust they become. When someone is standing within a victim storyline and is often telling that storyline of victimhood, to him- or herself and to others, it starts colouring thoughts, feelings and choices, and it has impacts on future experiences. When the person moves into a preferred storyline and begins to recount that storyline more than the problem storyline, it is possible to ask the person what difference this might make in his or her life. This opens up possibilities and considerations about how to act in the future, if people are guided by their preferred storyline.

White and Epston (1990) have suggested that 'only a fraction of [a person's] experience can be storied and expressed at any one time, and that a great deal of lived experience inevitably falls outside of the dominant stories about the lives and relationships of persons' (p. 15). They go on to say that it is within those events that have previously been un-storied that we can find a 'fertile source for the generation, or re-generation of alterative stories' (p. 15). They refer to these newly re-discovered events as 'unique outcomes', drawing on Goffman's (1961) work.

I have been asked at times if this process of shifting the focus from a problem storyline to alternative possibilities shares anything in common with the cognitive restructuring and reframing that is encouraged in cognitive behaviour therapy (CBT). Some cognitive restructuring may in fact occur, but this is not the focus of narrative therapy, and there is no attempt necessarily to encourage someone to look at a particular event in a different way. Rather, the conversation maps, and the re-authoring conversation map in particular, will assist people in paying more attention to those other events outside of the events that have formed their primary problem storyline.

During the years in which I have been interested in narrative practices and have focused on the conversation maps as a method of purposefully practising and further developing my skills in narrative practice, I think I may have inadvertently downplayed the importance of the literary and text analogy that White and Epston first described in 1990. Epston (2012) has also stressed the need to consider continually what makes for a rich and engaging story. In particular, he encourages us to consider developing the types of questions that are more apt to engage people's imaginations and curiosity in finding those previously un-storied events (unique outcomes) and creating new preferred ways of thinking about their lives.

Returning to White and Epston (1990), it is interesting to see just how much this notion of 'literary merit' (p. 17) was important in the beginning stages of the development of narrative therapy. They say:

When unique outcomes are identified, persons can be invited to ascribe meaning to them. Success in this ascription of meaning requires that the unique outcomes be plotted into an alternative story or narrative. And in this process, as acknowledged by Victor Turner (1986), 'imagining' plays a very significant role. Various questions can be introduced that assist in engaging persons in this ascription of new meaning, questions that actively involve them in, as Myerhoff (1982) would put it, the 're-authoring' of their lives and their relationships. ... In considering therapy as a context for the re-authoring of lives and relationships, I have proposed a 'therapy of literary merit' (White, 1988). (White and Epston, 1990, pp. 16–17)

Keeping in mind that White (1988), White and Epston (1990) and Epston (2012) have stressed this notion of literary merit, as well as having described the specific pieces that constitute a storyline, is important and reminds us of the artistry, as well as the science, of therapy and social work. As White (2007a) points out, however, the primary authorship of these stories does not reside within the therapist, but rather belongs to the people sharing those problem and alternative storylines.

Landscape of action and landscape of identity

White has pointed out (2005, 2007a) that although a storyline is made up of a series of events linked over time according to a plot or theme, if that was all a story was made up of, then it would be a pretty dull and un-engaging story. Drawing on Jerome Bruner's work, White (2007a) suggests that a story contains both a landscape of action and a landscape of identity. In earlier work White refers to a landscape of action and a landscape of consciousness, which was how Bruner described them, but to avoid confusion about what he was referring to, White changed the wording over time. He says:

> In describing the relevance of these concepts to the therapeutic practice I have substituted the term *identity* for *consciousness*. I made this substitution because of the confusion that arose around my use of this term. At times, the mention of consciousness was taken to denote an awareness of injustices. At other times this term was taken to denote the mechanism of the mind that is engaged when making choices. At yet other times it was taken to denote actions in life that were conscious in contrast to actions that were products of 'the unconscious.' (White, 2007a, p. 81)

The 'thicker' and more meaningfully engaging stories will not only be made up of the events regarding who did what, when and where, but will also have a richness to them based on an interweaving of hopes, dreams, intentions, values and preferences; this will also contribute to making the stories more engaging. This is true of the stories that people tell in practice also. People may not always be explicit about their hopes, dreams and values when telling their stories, but in order to assist them in becoming clearer about these elements we can ask questions like: 'The fact that you responded that way, what does that suggest is important to you?'; 'What is it that you were hoping for?'; or 'What would you say you value, given the fact you did that?' I remember White (2006) once saying that he would, at times, ask parents if they ever found themselves acting against their better judgement. How many of us could, in fact, answer that we've never acted against our better judgement? Not many, I think. If the parents had become accustomed to being investigated and held accountable for neglect or abuse of their children, and had spent much of their time focusing on the problem storyline within the landscape of action, then this simple question of White's could offer the opportunity to move into the landscape of identity. If they were able to acknowledge that they had from time to time acted against their better judgement, it would be possible to ask how their better judgement would have suggested they behave, if there had been any times when they had acted in accord with their better judgement and preferences, and who and what might support them in doing so again in the future.

If, when discussing the problem storyline, a person begins to remember an event that is inconsistent with the problem storyline, which may be the beginning of an alternative storyline, it is important to remember that a storyline is made up of more than just one event. It will be necessary to ask the sorts of questions that would help the person remember other events to link together with the newly remembered event, perhaps starting by asking the person to think back in time about how he or she had prepared for that 'new' event (Russell et al., 2006). It is also important to try to remember not to become so caught up in solely the facts that we only ask questions that would thicken the landscape of action of the new storyline. The story becomes more meaningful and robust, with more chance of continuing effects in the future, if it is thickened through details in the landscape of identity as well. This is a time at which I might resort to telling people that I am going to ask a silly question. These alternative storylines sound much more pleasant and seem like they are in line with the person's preferred way of living, but it is important, however, not to assume. It is helpful to ask the person about this and invite the person to be more explicit about what it is he or she prefers. I might say something like: 'This may sound like a silly question, but it sounds like you prefer acting according to your better judgement and being more patient with your child, but what is it that you prefer about that? Why do you prefer that?' As the person becomes more explicit about these hopes, dreams, values and preferences, the storyline becomes stronger and more resistant to negative influence.

The fluidity and social construction of identity

Social workers, and many other counsellors and therapists, are trained to consider the individual within his or her environment. This focus on the person within environment suggests that we cannot only consider the person's problems as being caused by some sort of individual flaw, but as having developed within a family, and a social and political context. The discourses to which a person has access will also influence interpretations and meaning-making. Whether a person lives in an inner-city housing project versus a rural setting obviously also has an impact on the person's attitudes and way of life. It is, therefore, not difficult to imagine the social construction of people's stories. Although we can conceive of stories being made up of a series of events linked over time according to a plot or theme and also being made up of both a landscape of action and a landscape of identity, it is useful also to remember that the shape of these stories shifts and take on slightly different meanings and importance as they are told to other people, as those people react, and as discourses are negotiated.

This is another reason why White believed the term 'landscape of identity' to be more useful than 'landscape of consciousness' in relation to narrative practices. He says:

> The term *landscape of identity* does have benefit in the emphasis that it gives to the significance of the therapeutic endeavour – it emphasizes the irreducible fact that any negotiation of the stories of people's lives is also a renegotiation of identity. Awareness of this encourages a fuller engagement on behalf of therapists with the sort of professional ethics that are associated with an acknowledgement of the life-shaping aspects of therapeutic practice and a greater awareness of the responsibility that we have for what we say and do in the name of therapy. (White, 2007a, p. 82)

As previously indicated, White and Epston's approach to therapy was very much influenced by their reading of Foucault, Derrida and Deleuze. White and Epston (1990) particularly focus on Foucault's understanding of the effects of knowledge and power on the construction of people's sense of identity. Rather than the common proposition that power is controlling in its negative and repressive operations, what interested White and Epston in the development of narrative practices was Foucault's focus on how 'power is constitutive or shaping of persons' lives' (White and Epston, 1990, p. 19). They say:

> [W]hen discussing 'truths,' Foucault is subscribing not to the belief that there exist objective or intrinsic facts about the nature of persons but instead to constructed ideas that are accorded a truth status. These 'truths' are 'normalizing' in the sense that they construct norms around which persons are incited to shape or constitute their lives. (White and Epston, 1990, pp. 19–20)

White (2007a) has also argued, based on Foucault's accounts of the rise of modern power, that these 'normalizing judgements' began to replace moral judgements as a form of social control in the seventeenth century. This, combined with the development of the concept of a 'self' as an essence that is believed to be at the centre of a person's identity, and the development of humanist beliefs in the existence of a 'human nature', contributed to the development of certain socially constructed 'truths' that started becoming taken for granted at the beginning of the twentieth century. These taken-for-granted 'truths' that were constructed and supported through mechanisms of power and knowledge had to do with internal states and intra-psychic mechanisms. White suggests, 'Over the past century, these internal state understandings of human expression have become pervasive in Western culture … [and] have achieved a taken-for-granted status in much professional and popular psychology' (White, 2007a, p. 102). I have written elsewhere (Béres, 2009), in my discussions regarding mindfulness and reflexive practice, that Buddhist and Eastern notions of the 'self' are quite different from Western taken-for-granted notions about the 'self', which assists with the process of realizing the social construction of these very ideas about self and identity.

As opposed to 'internal state' conceptions, White points out that 'intentional state' conceptions of identity are distinguished by the concept of 'personal agency': 'This concept casts people as active mediators and negotiators of life's meanings and predicaments, both individually and in collaboration with others' (White, 2007a, p. 103). Through considering intentional states, versus internal states, and privileging personal agency and decision-making over human nature, I have found that people discover a greater sense of hope in bringing about change in their lives; they are no longer trapped by thoughts of 'this is just how I am'.

White indicates (2007a) that people who seek, are referred or mandated to attend social work or counselling services often believe that the problems they are experiencing in their life are associated somehow with their identity: 'I can't help it, I'm just an angry guy'; 'This is who I am. I am an addict'; 'I have "V" for "Victim" stamped on my forehead. Men just know they can abuse me and I won't know how to stop it.' When the problem is described in these ways, and when therapists inadvertently use the language and assessments that diagnose and label, then the one aspect of the person's life that is the problem becomes described as if it totalizes the person's identity. That is why narrative therapists are careful and precise with language and find that it is much more productive and useful to talk about 'a man who has used abuse or abusive behaviours' and 'a woman who has experienced abuse' instead of 'an abuser' and 'an abused woman'. These last two terms totalize these people so that his identity is only that of an abuser and her identity is only that of a victim. These accounts also run the risk of pathologizing people so that they must somehow be sick and not 'normal' to be in this kind of relationship, not being able to control anger and abuse and not being able to protect herself. If a practitioner has discussions with the man about the effects of his choices to use abuse against his intimate partner, the practitioner is able to interact with him so that he is not totally and completely an abuser and nothing else, but rather someone who has learned these behaviours and can learn to privilege other preferred ways of being; this practice opens up choice and possibility.

The re-authoring conversation map

What most interested me in narrative practices when I was first introduced to them was the idea of externalizing conversations, particularly in moving away from pathologizing and totalizing accounts of people's problems. I was drawn to the idea of externalizing the problem and looking, for example, at the effects of anorexia or disordered eating in someone's life rather than focusing on the person as 'anorexic'. Much has been written about this approach with people regaining their lives from the control that anorexia had on them (Maisel, Epston & Borden, 2004).[7] So, for some time, I shared a common misconception about narrative practices, which was that an externalizing conversation was the most important and most unique skill of narrative practitioners. However, when I began more focused study of narrative practices at the Dulwich Centre, Shona Russell helped me understand that as narrative therapists we may not always need to engage in externalizing conversations, but we are in fact almost always re-authoring with people. That is why I think it is important to begin by describing a re-authoring conversation map in this introductory chapter before moving on to the more structured conversation maps in the next chapter.

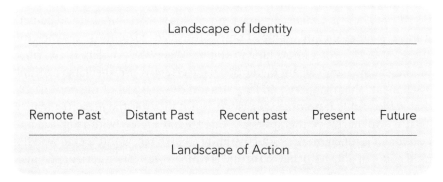

Figure 1.1 Re-authoring conversation map

Source: Adapted from White's 'Workshop Notes' posted on www.dulwichcentre.com.au

When I was first attempting to develop my skills in narrative practice, I would often draw the re-authoring conversation map on a piece of paper in order to help me remember the ideas inherent in the map. I would then take notes on the map as I met with people in therapeutic conversation, which would provide a picture of their storylines. As the map depicts, stories have a timeline from the remote past, through the distant and recent past, into the present, and carry implications for what can be expected in the near future. The map also depicts the two landscapes: one of action and the other of identity. By taking notes on the map, I also had a reminder right in front of me to move between the two landscapes, remembering the need to ask about values, hopes and dreams as well as about the details of what had happened. The notes and storylines will look wonderfully messy, since it is expected that conversations will cross back and forth between the two landscapes many times; and will also jump backwards and forwards along the timeline, as people remember various events in time, make links to future possibilities and respond to further questions.

White has depicted how it is possible to chart a re-authoring conversation in *Maps of Narrative Practice* (2007a). In fact, he has also, in that same text, charted therapeutic conversations demonstrating externalizing conversations, re-membering and outsider witnessing conversations. I have left the conversation maps blank in this text in order to encourage readers to make their own use of them. It can be helpful to practise by imagining how you might plot your own stories on a re-authoring conversation map, for instance, and consider how many storylines and zigzags are possible as you consider the significance of events and implications of hopes and dreams. It is possible for readers to take the ideas of these maps and develop their own ways of making use of them, as another form of 'copying that originates' (White, 2006).

In order to indicate the manner in which the re-authoring map can contribute to practice, the following case example has been provided by a social worker, Diane, working in child protection, who has incorporated the philosophy, ethics and skills of narrative practice into her work.

Practice example

Brenda had just given birth to a full-term baby girl.
Initial drug testing was positive for THC
(tetrahydrocannabinol, the principal psychoactive
constituent of cannabis) and the file history reported
that Brenda had struggled with alcohol and cocaine
addictions, anxiety and depression, and had lived a lifestyle
of transience for the previous nine years. Furthermore, police had
also recently been involved with Brenda and her previous
boyfriend, who was the possible father of the newborn baby, due
to a domestic dispute.

Case
study

My initial meeting with Brenda occurred prior to her release
from hospital with her baby. She presented as polite and
cooperative, but clearly anxious. She had lost her first-born child
in a custody and access dispute nine years earlier and was very
aware of the authority that came with my position.

My assessments with individuals are simple; I do not attempt to
trick or manipulate, but to be as transparent as I am able.
Following introductions, I read the report I had received, which
had triggered the involvement of child protection services, only
screening out to avoid disclosing identifying information, as I
know that individuals are anxious to know what has brought me to
their family. It is from there that dialogue starts. I remind people
that they are the experts on themselves and their children and
allow them to educate me regarding the dynamics within their
home. When I am confused, I ask questions to clarify.
Furthermore, I often tell families that the referral reports I receive
are only a small piece of a much bigger puzzle, and it is through
the discussions with family and community members that this
puzzle piece is put in its place and a much larger picture and
understanding emerges.

I followed this same pattern with Brenda and she was able to
answer each question in a manner that allowed me to believe
that she had been successful in addressing a number of the
presenting concerns over the course of her pregnancy. However,
it was agreed that given her history, the Children's Aid Society
would remain involved to demonstrate to the Ministry that the
presenting concerns had been mitigated, to support her in her
success as a mother, and to assist with connecting with
appropriate services.

After the initial meeting, I asked Brenda if she would be willing to tell me more of *her* story – not the story in the referral. I didn't want our relationship to be totalized by the presenting concerns of addictions and mental health, but rather wanted them to be placed within their proper context of her greater story. I was amazed when she told me that no one had ever asked this of her before, and even more amazed when she later revealed that she had told me parts (unique outcomes) of her story of which she had never before spoken; I was, after all, her child protection worker.

Our discussions followed the roadmap of a re-authoring conversation. As she started with her childhood, I attempted to gather a better understanding of her views and understanding of her experiences. I was cautious not to use my 'lens' to interpret or play the expert to these events, but rather asked questions like: 'Was that a good thing, a bad thing, or neutral?' and 'What made that experience significant for you?' While lingering in the landscape of action, she was able to speak of her relationship with her mother in honest and complex ways, seemingly without worries about my opinion.

Her vivid accounts of this time in her life allowed her to articulate clearly what this demonstrated that she valued and to move to the landscape of identity. She reported that she wanted to behave in a manner that was different than that of her mother in her childhood, stating that she valued mothering in a manner that demonstrated consistency, stability, boundaries and protection. She reported with pride that she was able to provide this to her first born during the first couple of years of his life prior to the custody dispute with his father. Her values were again strengthened and expanded on after reflecting on this period. It was this discussion that allowed her to articulate to me the values she wished to build on while parenting her newborn.

Although the Children's Aid Society entered the relationship with the 'mandate' to address the child protection concerns, it is her own values that will allow for true growth. They are ones that hold deep meaning to Brenda and will carry her forward towards far greater goals than those that could have been articulated by 'minimum community standards' as mandated by the Ministry or any goals that I could have suggested.

Diane's example of working with Brenda shows how she was able to use her expertise in relationship-building and narrative practice skills to privilege Brenda's expertise regarding her own life. She was able to use her authority ethically and respectfully, without abdicating or attempting to hide the power she has as a child protection worker. She used her power to empower Brenda to think about and make choices in her life. Diane's description of working with Brenda also shows how easily she could have become stuck in her focus on just the problem storyline, which was presented in past recording and in the referral. She took the problems seriously, but also engaged Brenda in thinking about where this problem storyline was situated in the rest of the events and storylines of her life. It is perhaps not surprising to read that Brenda indicated it was the first time any child protection worker had been interested in the rest of her life. It is within the rest of her life that an alternative storyline had its beginnings and provided Brenda with some hope about how she could reach her goals for mothering her new child.

Conclusion

As is probably clear by now, I am committed to the philosophical, political and ethical underpinnings of narrative practice. These are the elements that have inspired me and keep me motivated to continue to practise, research and teach this practice approach. I have presented these ideas in this first chapter because I think they are the most important aspects of this work. I have also described the basic elements of a storyline and the aspects of a re-authoring conversation that provide the framework for assisting people in moving from a problem storyline to an alternative and preferred storyline. As I move on to describe the other more structured conversation maps in the following chapters of the first part of this book, I hope that readers will engage with them within the context of these beginning thoughts on ethical relationships and therapeutic posture; fluidity and the social construction of identity; and the privileging of the values and hopes of those people who consult narrative practitioners. Keeping in mind these more philosophical commitments ensures that the use of the conversation maps does not become rigid and mechanical. The therapeutic relationship, and the people engaged in conversations, are more important than the conversation maps, yet the maps provide a structure for learning how to put otherwise abstract ideas into a useful practice with people.

Notes

1. www.neighbouringcommunities.net presents an overview of our team's work in the communities experiencing the effects of a land claim/rights dispute and the

ongoing effects of that initial community work in which we were involved with Michael White.

2. Barreto & Grandesso (2010); Denborough (2008); Denborough, Freedman & White (2008); Waldegrave et al. (2003) and White & Denborough (2005). The *International Journal of Narrative Therapy and Community Practice* also publishes many articles regarding community practices and creative integrations of narrative therapy.

3. Some readers may prefer to begin with the later section regarding elements of story and then return to this section.

4. These conversation maps are not crucial for practising narrative therapy and David Epston has not reviewed the maps in the training I have attended that he has facilitated (Epston, 2009, 2012).

5. I am thinking particularly about the sometimes dense and difficult writing of philosophers like Derrida, Deleuze and Foucault.

6. Tuhiwai Smith (1999) and Wilson (2008) have both been helpful in thinking through these issues.

7. Also see http://www.narrativeapproaches.com for further resources.

8. Diane completed the narrative therapy elective I teach in a university graduate social work programme and since then has been attending the narrative therapy consultation group I facilitate. She has guest lectured in a class I teach in the undergraduate university social work programme, inspiring and encouraging students that they can engage ethically and respectfully with people who are mandated to child protection services.

2 The Conversation Maps

Introduction

David Epston recently reminded me that Michael White often used the analogy of learning how to play jazz when he described the process of learning and developing skills in narrative practices. Epston highlighted an exchange between Michael White and Salvador Minuchin in which Minuchin admonished White for not talking enough about what he actually *did* in therapy. White responded by explaining that he felt it was more important to teach people how to play scales before they could improvise like a jazz musician. In fact, it would appear as though White spent a great deal of time reflecting on what he was actually doing in his practice so that he could break it down into small steps and make it easier for people to learn. In a way, he was talking about what he did in therapy when he described the conversation maps, although his interactions with people were much more fluid than the maps might initially imply.

As I indicated in the previous chapter, some students and colleagues have, at times, mentioned to me their frustration with White's conversation maps, because they seem to react to them as if they are rigid and directive of their interactions with people. I, and many others, have nevertheless found them extremely helpful both for learning how to practise from a narrative therapy perspective and for teaching how to practise. When watching White in a therapeutic conversation, or interacting with people within a community project, his questions and skills of engagement could seem simple in their ability to assist people in making much-hoped-for changes in their lives, and yet frustratingly difficult to replicate. Of course, he was not perfect and he shied away from others' attempts to suggest that he was, or equally from any suggestion that he was merely naturally gifted in his interactions. It may have been an attempt on his part to move away from these accounts that led him to develop the maps in order to show and teach people pragmatically what he was doing. It was not just some innate skill with which he was born that led to these profound interactions; he had developed a method of operationalizing his philosophy and politics of life into an ethical way of working with people. Swimming against the current of mainstream pressures about what it means to assess or diagnose and provide interventions to people is no easy feat. Rather than each one of us needing to re-invent the wheel while trying to find our own ways of operationalizing the philosophers' insights into practice, White reviewed his own practice in order to be able to describe clearly what he was doing. He did not expect us to practise these maps rigidly and, as I have already suggested, I have heard him say at the end of conferences that he was always interested to hear how others would take a narrative approach and make it their own.

I have previously described Schön's 'reflecting-on-action' and 'reflecting-in-action' (Béres, 2009; Duvall & Béres, 2011) and how useful his approach is for reflecting on our own practice in order to describe it, learn from it and develop it further. Fook and Gardner (2007) have further refined Schön's approach by adding an element of *critical* reflection, so that in reflecting in and on our practice we are also able to reflect on the effects of power and make connections to social and cultural discourses and understandings. (I will describe this in more detail in Chapter 6.) White appears to have engaged in a similar process in the development of his practice, and then the analysis and description of his practice, for training purposes. Schön (1983) was responding to a mistrust in how professional practice was being taught at that time, and also a mistrust in the scientific rational approaches to inquiry and theory development, which appeared to be coming from the 'top down'. The concerns he recognized in the professions and to which he responded are similar to concerns that many professionals have today. He wanted to honour the skills, intuition and artistry of professional practitioners and provide a method for them to reflect-*on*-action (think about what they had done after they had done it) and reflect-*in*-action (think about what they were doing as they were doing it and note how they responded to issues as they arose). This created a bottom-up method for the development of practice theory, which I believe is similar to what White and Epston (1990) have done in developing narrative therapy. They incorporated influences from a range of philosophers and anthropologists, but then each of them developed their own style of practising narrative therapy by reflecting on their practices further and gathering people's reactions about whether these practices had been useful to them. Through these reflections, White developed the conversation maps, which as has been noted are useful structures for learning how to practise narrative therapy.

Although I have not read anywhere that White was directly influenced by Schön, he has been explicit regarding the influence of Lev Vygotsky and his concept of the 'zone of proximal development'. Vygotsky's understanding and description of how children learn contributed to White's development of his conversation maps, which help structure therapeutic conversations so that people can learn and make the changes they want to make, but also so that beginning narrative therapists can learn how to structure narrative therapy interactions. White says:

> Vygotsky also emphasized that learning was an achievement not of independent effort, but of social collaboration. In this social collaboration, he observed that adult caretakers and more sophisticated peers structure children's learning in ways that make it possible for them to move from what is known and familiar to them and from routine achievements to what it is possible for them to know and achieve. He described this as a movement across a zone of learning that he termed the 'zone of proximal development.' This zone is the distance between what the child can know and achieve independently and what is possible for the child to know and achieve in collaboration with others. (White, 2007a, p. 271)

He goes on to describe the manner in which people who teach assist with the 'scaffolding' of the learning and the movement from what is already known to what it is possible to learn. At the time, Vygotsky's theories were in opposition to the taken-for-granted understandings of how children acquired skills, since it was generally understood that children naturally developed and learnt, rather than having behaviours and knowledge modelled and developed through social collaboration. This notion regarding the social collaboration involved in learning and making changes can also be noted in adults. As described in the previous chapter, if we do not ask the sorts of questions that facilitate reflection and the remembering of events that have not been previously recounted, the person recounting the problem story is very likely to continue to retell that problem story since it is known and familiar. It is through asking careful questions that possibilities are opened up and people can make choices based on their preferences and values.

When I have described the scaffolding of learning new skills and behaviours from the known and familiar to the possible to know, I have, at times, used the example of teaching a child how to brush his teeth. It is not very helpful simply to fling a toothbrush and toothpaste at a child and expect him to know what to do. Rather, if the process of brushing teeth is broken down into the smaller steps that make up the activity, it is easier for the child to learn the new skill. Another example from the other end of the age spectrum comes to mind as I recently gave my 87-year-old mother an iPad so that we could start keeping in touch via email, and she could search for knitting patterns online and otherwise enjoy the wonders of the internet. (She especially enjoys 'funny animals' on YouTube.) It would not have been particularly helpful merely to give her the iPad and expect her to know what to do with it. We have practised going in and out of the various apps (obviously a whole new language is being learnt as well) and she took note of the various smaller steps required of each activity. Together, we scaffolded her learning from what was already familiar to her to what she was actually able to learn with assistance, which she could not have figured out on her own.

Conversation maps provide the steps for scaffolding people's learning in therapeutic conversations from what they are already familiar with in their lives to a place where they are able to live their lives more in keeping with their preferences and hopes and have developed the skills and behaviours to maintain those changes. These conversation maps also, however, scaffold learning for the practitioner who wants to develop narrative practices. Once the narrative therapist has traversed the zone of proximal development him- or herself, from what was already known and familiar about his or her practice to what it is possible to know about narrative practices, the therapist does not necessarily need to use the conversation maps rigidly, but rather will have integrated the philosophy, politics and general skills of working narratively, and the maps will have been woven more fluidly into his or her work.

I will describe three conversation maps that White developed and described thoroughly in *Maps of Narrative Practice* (2007a). Unlike the re-authoring conversation map presented in the previous chapter, these conversation maps represent conversations as moving, if graphed, from the bottom of the page and what is already known and familiar, through four steps, to the top of the page and what it is possible to know. Two of the maps are externalizing conversation maps. The first of the externalizing conversation maps is also described as a statement of position map 1, and is regarding the problem in a person's life that may have been internalized, totalizing and pathologizing the person's sense of identity, and can therefore be externalized. The person is asked to make a statement about their position in relation to the problem. The second externalizing conversation map is described as a statement of position map 2, and is regarding the new skill or initiative that the person may be developing. The third conversation map I will describe is a re-membering conversation map and has to do with examining the effects of people in one another's lives; this is based on using the metaphor of a club, or association, that has members and membership. If we were to think of our lives as clubs, and people in our lives as having membership in our clubs of life, we can make decisions about who we want to give lifetime memberships to and from whom we might want to revoke membership altogether. White (2007a) also describes the outsider witnessing conversation map, which can be used in clinical types of therapeutic settings where teams of practitioners or students and trainees can be assigned as witnesses to therapeutic conversations, as well as in community projects and practices. When it is possible to integrate outsider witnessing, this conversation map can be very helpful for providing a greater social context to the practice, but I have found that most practitioners do not have the chance to integrate this map into their ongoing practice, so I will not describe the map in detail here, but in Chapter 5 when I describe agency-based practice, since it also provides a useful framework for engaging in consultation with other practitioners in team settings.

Bowles (in Béres, Bowles & Fook, 2011) has pointed out her view that the use of the word 'maps' to describe the structure of narrative conversations is inconsistent with post-modern influences, because post-modern geographers would certainly suggest that these structures are not maps. I agree that these 'maps' would more accurately be called 'lists of steps', 'charts' or 'graphs'. Although White (2007a) writes about maps of narrative practices, he does not include conversation maps in the manner that I am including them here: as blank structures that can be used to remind beginning practitioners of the possible steps in various types of conversations. He, rather, has charted the flow of conversations onto graphs, showing the manner in which a conversation is able to move up from one series of questions to the next, or perhaps will need to return to a former series of questions and then move up again. Each of the conversation maps that I present can be used to assist in structuring conversations, imagining moving during the time of the conversation, from the bottom left-hand corner of the graph up to the top right-hand side of the page; the x-axis of the graph could be considered the time passing within the conversation and the y-axis the various steps of the conversation.

Externalizing conversation (statement of position map 1)

As indicated in Chapter 1, the externalizing conversation is one of the approaches within narrative practices that perhaps most distinguishes it from other practice theories and so is often thought of as the most important conversation map. However, as I also pointed out in that chapter, I believe that the re-authoring conversation map and ideas about the social construction of identity through the telling of stories about events in our lives are also extremely important and defining of narrative practices. Externalizing conversations, for example, have been integrated in a manualized family-based treatment approach for treating anorexia (Ellison et al., 2012), but have been tagged on as another exercise to use with people rather than as part of an overall commitment to shift the politics and philosophy of the therapeutic approach.

In *Maps of Narrative Practice* (2007a), White begins his first chapter with a description of externalizing conversations. He does this because he says that many people seek therapy believing that the problems in their lives are due to a problem of their identity, others' identity or the identity of their relationships. He says, 'In short, people come to believe that their problems are internal to their self or the selves of others – that they or others are in fact, the problem' (p. 9). In a clear and succinct manner, White summarizes the importance of externalizing conversations:

> Externalizing conversations can provide an antidote to these internal understandings by objectifying the problem. They employ practices of objectification of the problem against cultural practices of objectification of people. This makes it possible for people to experience an identity that is separate from the problem; the problem becomes the problem, not the person. In the context of externalizing conversations, the problem ceases to represent the 'truth' about people's identities, and options for success-ful problem resolution suddenly become viable and accessible. (White, 2007a, p. 9)

I am saddened by how frequently I have heard people, even friends in casual conversations, describe what they consider to be core flaws within them-selves. They describe themselves as having attempted to change these flaws and yet they suggest that these problems are even more entrenched in their identity. Bracken (2012), in a lecture to a forum for existential psychology and therapy at the University of Copenhagen, suggests that since the mid-1700s and the rise of Enlightenment, which attempted to move people away from control by religion and instead towards a reliance on reason and science, there has also been an increasing focus on the notion of the individ-ual self, which was not at all common or taken for granted prior to that time. Drawing on the work of medical historian Roy Porter, Bracken goes on to describe how the Enlightenment's desire to control by reason led to the rise of asylums and the confinement of people whom society chose to exclude. He explains that although the profession of medicine started with the Greeks, the rise of psychiatry as a branch of medicine only began during the 1700s as a response to the need to deal with people who had been socially excluded and placed within asylums. He points out that in the twentieth century these assumptions about people have not disappeared, but rather have become even more reified. It is now a common-sense and taken-for-granted belief that problems are situated within individual selves and that we must control those individual problems that define the person; that which makes a person Anxious, a Depressive, an Abuser or a Victim, to give only a few examples of problems that can totalize a person's sense of self. These taken-for-granted 'truths' about how to think about people and prob-lems have been socially constructed.[1]

Using an externalizing conversation to help people examine the problems they are experiencing for how those problems are affecting their lives, rather than looking for causes of their problems within their identity, is not merely a useful and effective way of helping people develop ways of dealing with problems; it is also a political move, as we take a stand against 300 years of thinking about people as problems needing to be controlled.

As I have suggested, it is not necessary always to use an externalizing conversation with everyone we meet. In Chapter 3, for instance, I will review and describe the absent but implicit conversation map, which is used when people begin conversations by complaining about someone else or some other situation in their life. A general feeling that things have not been going well in life might be best discussed using a re-authoring conversation. It is when people present as having their identity totally described by a problem, or a diagnosis, that it is important to help them gain some distance from the problem so that they can see that there are other aspects to themselves and their lives besides the problem, even though it may have become all-consuming of their time and attention. Through having a conversation that allows people to examine the effects of the problem in their life, judge what they think about those effects and then consider why it is they judge the effects in those ways, they are able to see the problem as external from their sense of self. This means that they can begin to prioritize their intentions, rather than the internal under-standings, and can begin to make choices about how they would prefer to live in relation to the problem. The problem may not go away altogether, but they will have more control over it; and as their confidence in their skills over the problem increases, they may find the problem diminishing and dissolving further.

I have heard some people raise concerns about the notion of externaliz-ing the problem from the identity of the person because they confuse this approach with the idea of an external locus of control. If an internal locus of control is to be encouraged in people so that they take responsibility for their behaviours, in order to be accountable for the effects of their actions, an external locus of control, which might involve blaming others for their behaviours, will be seen as negative. Externalizing the problem, however, does not involve a shift to an external locus of control. In fact, if we are to think in terms of locus of control, externalizing the problem gives the person more control over the problem, not less. It is hard to change some-thing about yourself if you have started to think of it as 'just who I am', but a sense of control and choice is opened up when you can see that it is some-thing separate from your identity. These problems have often been shaped and influenced by social and popular discourses, and externalizing the problem assists the person in examining the context and history of the development of the problem, along with a reflection on who has been supporting the problem and who might support new behaviours (e.g. finding sponsors and mentors for clean and sober behaviours after a history of addiction).

In North America, and I believe this is also true in the United Kingdom, the diagnosis of attention deficit hyperactivity disorder (ADHD) is applied more and more frequently now than in the past. Once a child is labelled in this way, the diagnosis can result in other people thinking of that child *as* ADHD, rather than merely as *having* ADHD. This can result in parents and children at times giving up on attempts at making choices about how they would prefer to live together and interact, because the child's identity becomes totalized as ADHD, therefore he or she has no chance to be anything other than ADHD. I have at times worked with adults in counselling situations who have continued to describe themselves as ADHD. They have not necessarily initiated counselling because of this childhood diagnosis, but this sense of themselves as ADHD has continued to affect their sense of self, their relationships and their work.

To illustrate the use of the externalizing conversation map, I will describe a conversation I had with Joanne.

Action Plans · · · · · · · · · · · · · · · · · · · Possible to Know
_____

Justifying the evaluations · · · · · · · · · _____

Evaluating the effects · · · · · · · · · · · · _____

Describing the effects of the
problem · _____

Characterizing the problem
(experience near descriptions) · · · · · _____

· Known and Familiar

Figure 2.1 Externalizing conversation map (statement of position map 1)

Source: Adapted from White's 'Workshop Notes' posted on www.dulwichcentre.com.au

Joanne was referred to me after being fired from a job. She described herself as in between jobs and relationships and feeling anxious. In our first meeting, she told me how her mind always raced and how she thought this had resulted in her inability to perform well at work, which ultimately resulted in her losing her job. In the initial session I used the re-authoring conversation and, through this conversation, a problem story developed made up of a series of events about the manner in which her 'racing brain' had caused all kinds of trouble in her previous work positions and in past relationships. She then pointed out that she had been diagnosed as ADHD as a young teen.

Step 1: Characterizing the problem

Although in some situations when using a re-authoring conversation other events may be re-discovered that could lead to the development of an alternative and preferred storyline, when the conversation begins to focus instead on the identity of the person that is a clue that it might be more useful to shift into an externalizing conversation. If someone labels themselves as 'depressed', 'anxious', 'ADHD', 'obsessive-compulsive' or 'anorexic' rather than struggling with depression, anxiety and so on, it can be very helpful for the narrative practitioner to begin to shift his or her use of language and move into an externalizing conversation.

In addition to shifting the language away from 'being depressed' to 'living with the effects of depression', for instance, the first step of the conversation map involves externalizing the problem by talking about it as if it is a character in the person's life rather than as all-consuming of their identity. White has provided many examples of this approach when working with children, and it can be done quite playfully and creatively with young people. He has reported children responding well to talking about their ADHD as 'Mr Mischief', who causes all kinds of problems that the child begins to realize she does not like very much. I tend not to use such a playful approach with adults, although people are attracted to its creativity. With Joanne, I asked her when she had first been given the diagnosis of ADHD and then if she would describe what her ADHD was like, since ADHD can be different for different people. This involves what White describes as 'experience near descriptions' (White, 1994), because it moves away from global accounts and diagnostic language and begins the process of having the person describe the specifics of the situation and experiences with the problem.

Joanne said that she had been diagnosed early on and that she always felt different from most of her peers in the classroom. She said that she could not sit still and her parents tried to keep her busy with all kinds of sports in an attempt to try to tire her out. I pointed out that she had previously used the term 'racing brain' and I wondered whether that was another description of ADHD and whether that described what it was like. She said that it was a lot like racing brain and wiggly legs, since she could not sit still back then either. I asked, 'If we could call ADHD something more descriptive of what it was like in your life, what would you prefer to call it?' and she decided that 'racing brain' was closest to what it was like for her now. I asked if we could have a conversation about 'racing brain' in her life and she agreed that this might be a good idea.

It is often useful at this first step of the externalizing conversation to have an extended conversation about 'racing brain', or whatever experience near description of the problem is being used, in order richly to describe what it is like and to make it clear that this is not merely part of the person's identity. I sensed that Joanne had already become comfortable with this idea and that we could move on to the second step of the conversation map. If later on I had found that the conversation was becoming bogged down and she was finding it difficult to answer my questions, I could have moved back down the steps of the conversation map and asked her again to characterize the problem and describe what it was like in more detail. She might even at that point have decided to rename it in order to feel that she had developed a clearer description of it. It is a good idea to remember that, although the conversation maps are presented as a series of steps through which to move from the known and the familiar to the possible to know, at times it will be necessary to move back down to an earlier step before continuing on up to the possible to know.

Step 2: Describing the effects of the problem

I asked Joanne what she thought the effects of racing brain were in her life, and moved on to the second step of the map. The second step of the statement of position map 1 conversation involves asking about the effects of the problem in the person's life: on relationships and on the individual person. I asked Joanne if she was able and willing to describe some of what 'racing brain' did in her life. I said I was curious about whether 'racing brain' had any impacts on her relationships at school with her teachers and fellow students, whether it influenced her ability to concentrate on schoolwork and whether there were any effects at home or elsewhere. She was fully engaged with this conversation and had become curious herself in thinking back on the effects that 'racing brain' had had on her life and relationships. She said that 'racing brain' had kept her very energetic so she was always keen to be involved in sports, but that it, at times, had made her impatient with desk work and unable to concentrate, which then seemed to annoy her teachers. She said that she had made good friends on the sports teams and that her parents were supportive of this and protective of her from her teachers' negativity.

Step 3: Evaluating the effects

The third step of this conversation map involves asking the person to evaluate the effects of the problem. This is an important step, although practitioners new to these maps sometimes find it awkward to ask the person what they think about the effects just described. Beginning practitioners appear to judge for themselves and think that it is obvious that the effects are either negative or positive, and they often seem to feel nervous about appearing incompetent to the person with whom they have been speaking. It is useful, however, to remember to trust the process of this map and the underlying philosophy of narrative practices, which has to do with honouring the other person's expertise, knowledge and values over our own. People have surprised me by their evaluations, which are not always straightforward or expected. As often happens, Joanne, in answering my question about how she would judge the effects of 'racing brain' in her life ('Would you describe those effects as good, bad or a little bit of both?'), indicated that some of the effects of 'racing brain' were good and some not so good.

Step 4: Justifying the evaluations

In the fourth step of this map, people are asked to think about, and try to put into words, what their judgements about the effects imply is important and of value. Joanne had indicated that she did not like the fact that 'racing brain' affected her relationships with her teachers when she had trouble sitting still in class, but that she did, otherwise, appreciate her energy levels and the creativity that 'racing brain' seemed to bring about in her life. When asked to think about why she had judged one effect as not so good and the other as good, she articulated that she realized relationships were important to her, she thought there were difficulties with how the school system is structured, and she valued creativity and a healthy and active lifestyle.

Once the conversation has traversed the zone of proximal development and has moved from the known and the familiar to a place where values are clearer, it is possible to engage in a conversation about what difference it might make in people's lives if they were to remember the values that were uncovered in their judgements of the effects. Joanne realized that her preference for an active and creative lifestyle and holding on to that preference made it easier for her to think about what types of jobs she would prefer to apply for in the future.

Externalizing conversation (statement of position map 2)

Since there is a commitment in narrative practices to moving away from the language and conversations that could pathologize people through totalizing their identities to just the problem that brought them to counselling or social work services, it is also important to remember not to totalize people with a positive attribute either. Although the positive new skill, behaviour or attitude could indeed appear to be a good thing and would not necessarily pathologize people or make them feel bad about themselves, taking up a therapeutic or social work position that is informed by the narrative perspective involves consideration of the social construction and re-construction of identity, rather than a focus on internal strengths and weaknesses. It is important to centre the expertise and preferences of the person engaged in services and support the greatest amount of agency and choice for that person. Switching from a labelling of 'victim' to 'survivor' could be seen as more a matter of time and circumstance rather than choice, agency or intention. By making a commitment to remember to engage people in a statement of position map 2 conversation, which externalizes the new skill or preferred way of being, practitioners are able to assist people in developing a greater sense of control over their lives and identities. People are more than their problems and are also more than their positive new skills. In this way, they can develop a greater sense of their intentions, self-determination and efficacy in their lives.

The statement of position map 2 is very much like the statement of position map 1, but is in regard to the new skill or initiative rather than the problem.

By the end of the statement of position map 1 conversation with Joanne, she was clear that she was not ADHD but rather had experienced the effects of 'racing brain' in her life. Instead of her identity being limited by this diagnosis, she recognized that she was much more than that and was a person who had been affected by certain behaviours and issues. She had realized that she did not like the negative effects of this type of energy on some of her relationships and also that she valued creativity and a healthy and active lifestyle. This began to suggest possible job choices for her, since her main reason for commencing counselling was in order to reflect on her recent job loss and to think about what she might do next. As she thought about this more over the course of a few weeks, she began to see that she could actually harness the energy of her 'racing brain' and she started to describe this harnessing of her energy and enthusiasm as a new skill that she wanted to develop further. Working through the steps of the statement of position map 2 gave Joanne the time and structure to make this idea more concrete and detailed, and therefore easier to put into practice in her life.

Action Plan   Possible to Know

Justifying the evaluations   _____

Evaluating the effects   _____

Describing the effects of the
new skill or initiative   _____

Characterizing the new skill
or initiative
(experience-near descriptions)   _____

                                     Known and Familiar

Figure 2.2 Externalizing conversation map (statement of position map 2)
Source: Adapted from White's 'Workshop Notes' posted on www.dulwichcentre.com.au

Rather than slipping into discussions of creativity as if it were a positive trait she just happened to have internally, we were able to externalize it and characterize it as 'harnessed energy'. After doing this in the first step, I asked her to describe what the effects of harnessed energy were in her life. She said that at those times when she had harnessed energy in her life, she felt more in control, better able to focus and complete tasks, and yet still able to enjoy life. She said that further effects were that she felt better able to get along with people and try new things. She clarified that this was not about stifling her energy, or feeling dampened, but rather about being able to access, control and use her energy appropriately. Although that all sounded positive to me, it was not up to me to judge whether these effects were good or not, and so in the third step of this conversation I asked her what she thought about these effects in order to privilege her judgement. She said that she liked all of these effects and that she was feeling happier and more hopeful as a result of harnessing the energy.

Asking her to 'justify' these judgements, which is the fourth step of the conversation map, led her again to being able to articulate her personal values and preferences. As could be expected, some of the values and preferences she described were similar to those she described at the end of the statement of position map 1 externalizing conversation: a respect for relationships and an appreciation of creativity. Through reflecting on why she had judged being able to focus and get things done as a good thing, however, she became clearer about some other values. She thought back to her concerns about how the school system responds to children who have lots of energy and trouble sitting quietly at a desk focusing on work. She began to think that it was important for her to use her experiences and skills in helping other children appreciate their energy and not feel bad about themselves. This seemed to provide her with a great deal of motivation for helping children who were in similar situations to those in which she had found herself as a teen. The last I heard from her was that she was harnessing her energy and applying for positions where she would have the potential to assist children in such situations.

Re-membering conversations

Some of the most moving examples of re-membering conversations I have witnessed have been in relation to honouring and celebrating the contributions made to a person's life by someone who has died. White has written about this through the metaphor of 'saying hullo again' (1988). He also indicates that the development of the re-membering conversation was furthered through his engagement with Barbara Myerhoff's (1986) work. Her activities as a cultural anthropologist had focused on an elderly Jewish community in Venice Beach in California. In watching the documentary of her work in Venice Beach (Myerhoff, 2007), it is lovely to witness the manner in which otherwise frail and isolated elderly Jewish people are provided with a sense of community and more robust sense of their identity and contributions to one another through their involvement in one another's lives at a community centre. Myerhoff focuses on the significance of the re-membering of lives for people in that community and White takes up her approach in the therapeutic setting. He quotes Myerhoff as defining re-membering as 'a purposive, significant unification, quite different from the passive continuous fragmentary flickering of images and feelings that accompany other activities in the normal flow of consciousness' (Myerhoff in White, 2007a, p. 136). White goes on to say:

> This definition of re-membering evokes the image of a person's life and identity as an association or a club. The membership of this association of life is made up of significant figures of a person's history, as well as the identities of the person's present circumstances, whose voices are influential with regard to how the person constructs his or her own identity. Re-membering conversations provide an opportunity for people to engage in

a revision of the membership of their associations of life, affording an opening for their reconstruction of their identity. (White, 2007a, p. 136)

White explains how Myerhoff's approach, along with his 'saying hullo again' metaphor for working with grief, assisted in the development of the re-membering conversation for a variety of situations, after the realization that it was not only helpful in relation to grief.

Re-membering conversations in this case are not about remembering (recalling details), but rather about re-organizing memberships, hence the use of the hyphen. I have previously used the image of a golf or country club, but since I do not play golf, perhaps I would be providing an example closer to my interests if I were to use that of a yoga studio or gym instead. By thinking of my life as if it were like a gym, I can think of people in my life as holding memberships. Perhaps some people work in my gym while others have volunteer positions on my board of directors. Some have short-term or trial memberships and others have lifetime memberships. Although I might be extremely happy about the involvement of many of these people in my club of life, I might have also thought of myself as stuck with, and having to put up with, certain people. Through thinking of people's involvement in my life like a membership, and through examining the effects of their involvement on both my and their identity, I may choose to adjust the memberships. I might not want to go so far as to fire someone, or revoke a membership totally, but in celebrating and highlighting the positive impacts of some of the members, the role of other members can be diminished. For people who have experienced childhood abuse or domestic violence, it can be quite liberating and powerful to realize that they can elevate the impacts of some people and diminish the effects of those who have abused them.

The re-membering conversation, as it is structured on the re-membering conversation map, is used in order to elevate someone's role/membership in the life of the person engaged in conversation with the practitioner. Since the steps of this map heighten the importance of someone in the person's life, these steps are not useful when discussing someone who has had a nega-tive effect. Therefore, this conversation map is especially beneficial for people who are experiencing grief over the death of someone who was particularly special and important to them; or to detail further the two-way contributions of someone who has previously had a positive effect in the person's life; or to think about who might be of valuable assistance in supporting the person's new skills that have been developing. For example, when Brenda, in Diane's description of her work with her in Chapter 1, talked about her childhood and how she wanted to be a different type of mother than the mother of her childhood, it would be possible to ask Brenda who might be the least surprised to hear her talking like that. If she

Possible to Know

Person's contribution to figure's identity	_____
Person's contribution to figure's life *(actions)*	_____
Figure's contribution to person's identity	_____
Figure's contribution to person's life *(actions)*	_____

Known and Familiar

Figure 2.3 Re-membering conversation map
Source: Adapted from White's 'Workshop Notes' posted on www.dulwichcentre.com.au

was able, for instance, to say that in fact her aunt would not be surprised to hear her talking about wanting to be a different kind of mother, and that her aunt had filled some of her mother's role in her life, a re-membering conversation could provide an opportunity to think in more detail about how they could support one another in their preferred mothering skills.

For some people, particularly those who have lived through many years of trauma and many experiences of damaged and damaging relationships, it is difficult to think of anyone who has had a positive impact. In my experience, I have found that even people with an extensive history of abuse in their lives have been able to find at least one person who has offered a different experience. It might be that a person remembers one particularly kind teacher, a supportive and encouraging sports coach, or a pet, who helped them get through childhood. I have witnessed re-membering conversations being conducted in relation to the effect of a childhood dog and even that of a favourite teddy bear, where the person imagines what the pet or toy would have been thinking. I have not had the experience of a person not being able to think of anyone positive, but it is possible that a person's life could be this empty of positive supports, so this re-membering conversation can, in those situations, be used in regard to a public figure, author or character who is an inspiration for the person, even if they do not know each other. Then the questions can involve having the person think about what it might mean to the figure that he or she has had such a helpful influence if that figure were ever to be told.

I recently met for a series of sessions with Cheryl, who described herself as continuing to experience grief as a result of her husband Jeff's suicide three years earlier. She explained that she was continuing to feel angry that he had given up on both himself and their life together, but also frustrated by the manner in which friends and family were implying she should be over him by now and moving on in her life. This seemed like the sort of situation in which Cheryl might benefit from a re-membering conversation, to 'say hullo again' and hold on more firmly to the good memories and effects, rather than having to let go of all her memories. I asked Cheryl if she would like to talk more about Jeff and the effects of their relationship. She said that she was willing to give it a try, since she did not think it would make things worse and, in fact, she thought it might be helpful.

Step 1: The figure's contribution to the person's life

The first step of the conversation involves asking about what the figure (Jeff) contributed to the person's (Cheryl's) life in concrete ways. This shares something in common with the landscape of action in the re-authoring conversation, because these are the 'who', 'what', 'when' and 'where' details of the story of their time together. This first step involved asking Cheryl if she could talk about some of the things they did together, what they particularly enjoyed doing, and some of the ways she thought he contributed to her life. I could have asked her to share a small story to illustrate how their relationship and the things they did together made a difference to her. Cheryl described the beginning stages of their relationship when she and Jeff had met at university. She talked about how his commitment to his studies motivated her own studies and how a healthy type of competition developed, where they both wanted to do really well but supported and helped one another also. In addition, she described the two years of their marriage prior to Jeff's suicide as exciting, as they moved to a different city for their new jobs.

Step 2: The figure's contribution to the person's identity

The second step of the conversation suggests asking the person (Cheryl) to consider the way in which the figure (Jeff) and the figure's contribution to her life shaped her sense of herself and her life, which is like moving the conversation into the landscape of identity. I asked Cheryl what she thought

Jeff might have first noticed about her and appreciated about her. I asked her if she could imagine what it was that Jeff noticed about her that others maybe had not. I also asked if she could imagine seeing herself through Jeff's eyes and what he would say he most valued about her. She said that, although her classmates might have considered her boring and overly focused on her studies, Jeff valued her commitment, since they shared that in common. She said that he thought she was beautiful rather than just a bookworm and that he had recognized her adventurous side, which meant she was ready and willing to move and take a chance with a new city. This resulted in her feeling more confident.

Step 3: The person's contribution to the figure's life

Realizing how difficult it often is for people to talk about their own abilities and skills, since we are often told not to brag or be self-centred, it is helpful and reassuring to let people know how uncomfortable and difficult it can be to answer the next set of questions. Moving back from questions that share something in common with landscape of identity questions to those that are more concrete and more similar to landscape of action questions, the third set of questions ask people to think about what they did that contributed to the other's life. I warned Cheryl that it might be difficult and odd to think about these questions; however, I asked if she could think about what she had actually done in order to encourage Jeff's interest and contribution to her life. This type of question helps people realize that a relationship is never only one way and cannot come about merely because of the other person's actions. Jeff could have been the nicest guy she ever met at university and could have indicated his interest in her, but if she had not responded in an encouraging manner the relationship would not have had a chance. I asked: 'How did you respond to Jeff's appreciation of you?'; 'Could you describe some of the specific things you did to show Jeff you were interested in him?'; 'How do you think you contributed to Jeff's life?' These questions helped Cheryl focus on her own sense of agency and the effect that she and Jeff had had on the social construction of one another and their relationship. She realized that the fact that she was just as happy studying with Jeff as she was going out to the pub with him supported him in his work ethic. She thought that by paying attention to his attention, she demonstrated her interest in him. She believed that he probably felt just as good as she had about beginning to be appreciated by someone who also wanted to do well, and did not therefore think of him as boring and work driven. At the same time, however, she thought that it was probably good for him that she actually was happy also to go to the pub and find ways to integrate some more fun activities into their lives. She remembered, for instance, packing and organizing a picnic for them as a much-needed break from studying for exams and that, although he appreciated and enjoyed this, he probably would have merely kept on pushing himself if it had not been for her.

Step 4: The person's contribution to the figure's identity

The fourth step of this conversation map involves inquiring into what the person (Cheryl) thinks about the impact that her involvement in the other person's life had on shaping what he thought about himself and his life: his identity. The way this set of questions is asked is clearly somewhat different if the other person is still alive and the ongoing contributions can be considered. In Cheryl's situation, however, I asked her to think about what was made possible for Jeff because they had been together, and what she thought was probably different in his life because of her contributions. These types of questions can bring about some quite emotional and moving recognitions of the person's positive impact on the life of someone who was also very important to her. In Cheryl's situation, her range of emotions was that much more complex because she was not only able to see how she had had a positive effect in Jeff's life while he was alive, but was also furious that he had committed suicide and, in her way of thinking, chosen to leave her. What happened for Cheryl, through her reflections, was a growing awareness that Jeff could very well have been struggling for many years with an unrecognized mental health issue. She began to think that she had given him support for his study and his work, had brought some fun and happiness into his life, and that maybe he had managed his mental health for longer than he might otherwise have done if she had not been in his life.

I usually ask people at the end of any conversation if they have a sense of what was most useful from the conversation and what they think is most likely to stay with them and have an ongoing effect; it is especially important to ask something like this to finish the re-membering conversation. I asked Cheryl: 'If you were to remember your time with Jeff and the contributions you made to one another's lives more, what difference do you think that might make in your life now? Might that make anything possible for you in your life?' Cheryl thought that if she focused more on what she and Jeff had been able to contribute positively to one another, she would be able to remember the good times and let go of some of her anger towards him. She said that she would be able to think about the healthy and happy Jeff as an ongoing aspect of her life, and that she could even imagine consulting him from time to time when she wanted to think through decisions in her life. She also pointed out that although she appreciated the good intentions of her family and friends in advising her to let go of Jeff, she preferred this sense of being able to trust her intuition and hold on to good memories. She was beginning to feel positive about how much good she had done in Jeff's life, while also realizing that she did not have the power to control life and death.

Conclusion

I hope that by describing these three conversation maps I have provided examples of how to begin to structure conversations in such a way as to integrate complex post-modern and post-structural theories into practice. Even with a belief in the necessity of deconstructing discourses and the effects of social contexts, combined with an interest in the notions of multiple storylines, it is difficult to shift practice approaches without these conversation maps to provide some structure. This is because much of mainstream social work and therapeutic training does not necessarily provide a clear description of the types of questions and conversations that can assist people in uncovering some of these contextual influences. If a beginning narrative therapist has previously been trained in more traditional forms of counselling, and one of those forms of practice has become the primary professional storyline, it takes a concerted effort to shift to an alternative narrative practice storyline. Initially, if I did not keep the statement of position maps in mind, for instance, I too easily forgot to ask people to make their own judgements about the effects of problems in their lives, or did not remember to ask them what their judgements implied was important to them. The reason I was apt to forget to ask about these steps of the conversation is because my previous training in social work in an academic graduate social work programme encouraged, and privileged, the development of my insights in assessment over my practice skills in supporting the development of those insights in people consulting me. Good interventions with people are not those in which I demonstrate how clever I am at assessing and understanding their situations, but rather those in which I ask the kinds of questions that mean they can experience the insights, and begin to feel more confident in making their own decisions based on a clearer recognition of what is important to them. This also provides a method to support people's personal agency and sense of choice, while developing their confidence in their own skills and expertise, rather than developing a reliance on professional expertise. As I have indicated, it will not be necessary always to use these conversation maps to guide the structure of conversations with people, but they are a helpful support when initially learning to work narratively.

Note

1. See Foucault's *Madness and Civilization* (1965) and *Ethics* (1994) for full descriptions.

3 Exploring What Has Been Implied

Introduction

During the last training session I attended with Michael White in December 2007, he spoke to all of us present about the fact that he had begun to wish he had stressed much more the importance of 'the absent but implicit' in conversations, and that he was further developing and writing about the absent but implicit conversation map. He spoke of how he had realized how useful this concept and map were in assisting people in moving beyond their complaints and frustrations. He suggested that this was possible if the types of questions were asked that allowed people to start to reflect on the values that were underlying their complaints and were implicit in how they were describing their concerns. Since many people begin conversations with social workers and counsellors by complaining about other people or situations in their lives, this absent but implicit conversation can frequently be useful. White spent much of the training week discussing what he meant by 'absent but implicit' and having us practise this conversation with one another. Following his death just four months later, his close friends and colleagues took up the challenge and published their suggestions about the steps of an absent but implicit conversation map (Carey, Walther & Russell, 2009).

I have previously highlighted, in a chapter regarding the circulation of language within narrative practices (Duvall and Béres, 2011), White's contention about the importance of the philosophers Foucault, Derrida and Deleuze to the development of narrative practice; particularly Derrida and Deleuze to the development of the 'absent but implicit' concept within narrative conversations. Wyschogrod (1989) has described some of Derrida's contributions to the notion of the absent but implicit when stating, 'Representation conceals, while pretending to reveal' (1989, p. 191). Therefore it is important as practitioners not to limit ourselves to only the surface meaning of the words people use, but to explore the fullness of what might be meant by the words, and what also is implied by those words. This could be described as being a little like reading between the lines; however, it involves assisting the other person in reading between the lines so as to uncover what is implied by their statements, rather than making our own assumptions and interpretations. Wyschogrod goes on to explain:

> For Derrida … each element acquires meaning only through a play of differences, the intersignificative relationship to one another of elements which themselves lack self-present meaning. Each element is so inter-woven with every other that it is constituted only by the traces within it of the other bits in the chain or system. There are no independent mean-ings but only traces of traces. (Wyschogrod, 1989, p. 192)

This is a reminder of the social construction of identity and meaning not only within discourses, but also within each word used. When a person is attempting to describe complex emotions, thoughts and reactions, it becomes even more important to be cognizant of the multiple and fluid meanings of the words used. The word 'depressed', for example, will mean something different to each person using it, based on a range of experiences, and the meanings will also change over time. This is partly why it is useful to generate thick and detailed descriptions of the problem in the first step of an externalizing conversation statement of position map 1. Merely external-izing 'depression' may not be as useful as externalizing a person's description of what depression is like in his or her life.

Fisher and Augusta-Scott (2003) were the first to assist me in understand-ing the importance of moving beyond dualisms and into a greater comfort with fluidity and multiplicity of meanings, when they presented how impor-tant this movement is for working with men who have used abusive behav-iours in their intimate relationships. They pointed out how dualisms such as male–female, black–white or abusive–not abusive/passive set up conditions of choosing whether people are 'either one or the other', which is not partic-ularly useful in therapeutic conversations. Even yin and yang, which repre-sent dark and light (and masculine and feminine elements), are presented in the yin–yang symbol as more fluid than Western ideas of female and male often are. Thinking of the social construction of gender identity versus the physical sex of a child as he or she is born, it may be easier to realize that gender is perhaps more properly represented along a continuum, or as more fluid, rather than as two distinct and separate categories. This idea of moving away from dualisms is important when working with people for whom we are attempting to challenge totalizing and pathologizing accounts of their identity. As I pointed out in Chapter 1, if a man is labelled as abusive, rather than described as a man who has used abuse, he can find his identity totalized and his choices for alternative behaviours limited. He is, in fact, not only an abuser and he has acted in non-abusive ways at times in his life. He could not be labelled non-abusive either, however. More accurately, he might be positioned somewhere along the continuum of having used abusive–non-abusive behaviours and yet being able to learn new behaviours in order to move closer to the end of the continuum that could be labelled non-abusive.

Despite the fact that it is useful to move away from these dualisms and dichotomies in practice with people, it appears as though we might continue to think in opposites when we are using words to describe our thoughts and feelings. Derrida describes this in terms of each word (or 'signifier', as he also referred to it in *Of Grammatology* [1974]) involving both a description of what it is attempting to represent (the 'signified') and also a description of its opposite (or what it is not). Derrida referred to this idea of a word containing a comparison of what it is attempting to represent as 'différance' or difference. We might describe a certain food as 'bitter' and as we use that word it also contains within it the opposite of bitter, because we can only label our experience of something as being bitter because we have also experienced other tastes before. If the person who hears the word 'bitter' had only ever tasted bitter food, he or she might have difficulty understanding what 'bitter' means, or may not understand what the purpose of calling something 'bitter' would be. This would be due to the fact that there would be no other category with which to contrast it.

It was only when I first moved to North America that I heard what has now been described as an urban legend: that the Inuit have many different words for the English word 'snow'. I fell prey to this legend because it seemed to make sense. If someone rarely has any experience of snow, it might be enough only to have one word for snow and that person would know what snow is when it arrives and is different from the usual weather. When I began learning to ski, it was important to me not to ski on icy snow, since I had little enough control on skis as it was, without having to worry about the ice as well. I learnt about the difference between soft, powdery snow and wetter snow, which is heavy to shovel and great for making snowmen, but can slow you down too much on a ski slope. Our experiences shape our need for, and our understanding of, words, and by extension our ability to understand what another person means by the use of certain words. When living in the south of England, I needed more of an understanding of the different types of rain and wind than I did of the various types of snow.

In relation to social work and counselling conversations, if people have always been sad and listless and despairing, they may not complain about the condition because they have had no other experience against which to compare it. This means that when people talk about how much despair and hopelessness they are experiencing, we can be hopeful for them and listen for the experiences, even if in the remote past, that they have had against which they can compare these current concerns. If they know that they are experiencing despair and have labelled it as such, then there is 'différance' contained within that word and the possibility of assisting them in moving into a closer experience of happiness and contentment again.

Dooley and Kavanagh (2007) suggest that words, whether spoken or written, only ever partially represent what is being described. They explain that Derrida suggests that language is vulnerable and unable to encapsulate the truth or meaning of what it is attempting to label. Vulnerability suggests an openness, flexibility and negotiation of meaning.

Derrida's approach of deconstruction provides a method of taking apart and examining, or unpacking, all the possible influences and meanings held within a word. Deconstruction is often used in textual analysis, and I have been especially interested in deconstructing popular cultural texts that romanticize abuse. A woman who was meeting with me many years ago at the beginning of my career as a social worker told me that she was reading romance books to try to learn how to behave so that her husband would not beat her. I became fascinated and concerned by the romantic portrayal of abusive and controlling behaviours in intimate relationships in the media, and so began a study that involved interviewing women who had experienced abuse about their negotiation of the messages contained in popular cultural texts (Béres, 1999, 2001, 2002). I incorporated this approach into my work with men and women who had experienced abuse in their relationships, in order to assist them in externalizing the abusive behaviours and recognizing the social construction of these expectations, highlighting their personal agency and the possibility of choosing to learn different behaviours.

White incorporated Derrida's concepts directly into practice through his concept of 'double listening'. This notion suggests that not only does a word contain its opposite, the problem story or complaint also contains within it alternative or preferred stories. Practitioners need to be listening for possible entries into alternative stories, assisting people through the types of questions asked to consider what their values and preferences could be that are implied in the problem storyline. It is important to keep in mind that this is not done from a position of expertise or judgement about what that other story must be; it is done from a position that is curious about what the other person would say about the implications. An absent but implicit conversation is one type of conversation that provides a format for double listening when the 'presenting problem' is a complaint. As often is the case, this is easier said than done. When I first heard White discuss these ideas (2007b), he presented the absent but implicit conversation map as a series of eight steps, as have Carey, Walther and Russell (2009). I have wondered if with further work White might have simplified these eight steps and developed this conversation into another conversation map that could have been presented as four steps, moving from the known and the familiar to the possible to know, like the externalizing and re-membering conversation maps I have described in Chapter 2. I have found it clearer to position the eight steps that White (2007b) and Carey, Walther and Russell (2009) described into a framework that is more consistent with the four-step structure of the conversation maps.

Possible to Know

Move into a re-authoring conversation – linking this to the social and relational history of how these skills and preferences were learnt in the past and also what this might make possible for the future.

Justification _____

What was the purpose of doing this and what does this imply is important to you?

Link to knowledge and skills _____

How were you able to recognize 'disrespect' and how did you learn to 'stand up against it'?

Name and describe what you are doing in response

Possibly like 'taking a stand against disrespect'

Name and describe the main gist of the complaint

Possibly like the other person is disrespectful of me when he keeps on being late all the time

Known and Familiar

Begin by gathering the details of what the person wishes to discuss. If it is regarding a complaint about a person or situation, then this will be a clue that an absent but implicit conversation could be useful.

Figure 3.1   The absent but implicit conversation map.

Context and steps of the absent but implicit conversation map

Whether in a first meeting with someone or at some point during the course of engaging in conversations, it is not uncommon to hear the expression of a complaint, annoyance or discouragement. This stage of the conversation is a lot like merely asking people what they would like to talk about and realizing that they want to complain about something or someone else in their life. There have been many times over the course of my career before I became familiar with the absent but implicit conversation when I was left not quite knowing how to approach this sort of presenting problem, since the person causing the problem or complaint was not part of the social work conversation. I may have, at times, attempted problem-solving with the person who was in conversation with me, attempting to help them decide how to respond to the other person. This has never seemed particularly useful, as the conversations remained at the surface level of the behaviours rather than assisting people in becoming clearer about their own values and preferences, and stepping into a position of personal agency in regard to the problem and future potential problems.

It is important to gather the details of the story at this beginning stage, like thickening the problem storyline before moving into a re-authoring conversation and looking for alternative storylines. It could also be helpful to ask about the effects of the problems or behaviours that the person has been complaining about. There would, however, not necessarily be a need to name the problem at this point.

A simple example would involve a woman complaining about her brother always being late when they have agreed to meet:

> I hate that Joe is always late when we make plans to meet. He really bugs me. He's so rude. I may have rushed and made an effort to get there on time and then I end up waiting and waiting, twiddling my thumbs and getting more and more agitated the longer I wait.

If, rather than complaining about her brother, she focused on how angry she was generally, and the example of her brother was one of many ways in which she described herself as angry, this might suggest that an externalizing conversation would be more useful, allowing her to separate her identity from a potentially totalizing account of herself as an 'angry person'. If, however, she is complaining generally about another person rather than about her own anger, this would signal the usefulness of attempting an absent but implicit conversation.

Step 1: Name and describe the main gist of the complaint

The first step of this conversation, once it has been decided that the absent but implicit conversation might be the most useful conversation map to begin with, involves asking the kinds of questions to help people look for, and understand, what the ideas and beliefs are within the problem: to deconstruct what is contained within the problem and examine more fully what aspect(s) of the problem is causing the greatest amount of frustration. It may be useful to have people think about how they would name this main part of the complaint.

By asking the person who is angry about her brother always being late what she is standing up against, it is possible to externalize what is being reacted to, and, in doing so, assist her in becoming clearer about her own personal agency and worth. This helps move the conversation away from what she might minimize at times as being petty (e.g. 'Why do I get so worked up about him always being late?'), or away from a conversation characterized by blaming (e.g. 'He's awful to me. He's so disrespectful'), to a position where she can examine the implications of the problem and why it bothers her so much.

> He acts as though I don't matter and my time doesn't matter. In complaining about Joe being late I guess what I'm saying is that I don't like being disrespected. I don't think it's okay for him to minimize and disrespect me like this. I'm reacting to feeling as though he thinks my time doesn't matter because I'm not important.

Step 2: Name and describe the response to the main gist

The next step of the conversation map involves asking people to think about how they would describe, and perhaps name, their response to what they believe the other person is doing. Asking 'What word would fit what you are doing in response to what feels like diminishment and disrespect?' would be one way of going about this. This step is similar to the step in the externalizing conversation maps (statement of position maps 1 and 2) that involves characterizing and naming the problem (in statement of position map 1) or the new skill or initiative (in statement of position map 2). The person would not be complaining if she was 'going along with' what was happening, so what is she doing instead of 'going along with' it? It sometimes takes people a little more complaining before they are able to hone a more precise description of what they are doing. It might be helpful to ask whether they think they might be taking a stand against the treatment. As long as this suggestion is made tentatively, people will be able to disagree and offer alternative language to describe their actions.

I don't like feeling as though I'm not important enough for him to be on time. I'm disagreeing with his treatment of me. I'm saying it isn't right for him to be disrespectful. I'm **standing up** against the slight and I'm **speaking up** about what is important to me.

Step 3: Link to knowledge and skills

Since it is possible that some people would not mind waiting and would not see the brother's behaviour as a slight, it is useful to ask the people complaining how it is that they were able to recognize this situation as disrespectful and start to take some action by speaking up about it. I am reminded of one woman in particular who sent me an email asking if she could make an appointment to meet me. I responded and told her I could see her that week, but would then be out of the country for a couple of weeks, so if she preferred I could refer her to someone else. I was concerned that she may not want to start and then have to wait for me to return. Her response gave a hint of what was to become one of the issues she wanted to address in our conversations. She replied that she totally understood if I was busy and she did not want to be a bother. I explained that I was not too busy, and that she was not being a bother. I also suggested that we could meet and then stay in touch via email while I was away, if that would help. Over the first few meetings she began to describe how she had stopped standing up for herself as her husband's behaviours towards her and their child had become more and more controlling and emotionally abusive, and how her sense of worth had eroded due to these behaviours. At that point she probably would have waited for her brother if he was late every time and not complained, because she had become disconnected from her skill of standing up to people. As she has begun to complain about her husband's behaviours, now that they have separated and she is safe, she is reflecting back on her past behaviours and skills that she now wishes to re-develop. As she complains now, it is important for me to ask the sorts of questions that will help her put these skills into a context within her own history. This may be the beginning of putting this action into a storyline.

Going back to the example of the woman complaining about her brother, she suggested the following:

I guess this has bugged me about other people too and I've had to **stand up like this before**. I'm always very careful to be **on time for others**.

Step 4: Justification

As with the externalizing conversation maps (statement of position maps 1 and 2), the absent but implicit conversation map also has 'justification' as its fourth step. This has to do with asking why this reaction/behaviour in response to the gist of the complaint is important. Sometimes simply asking 'Why is this so important to you?' may provide some useful reflections. At other times, 'What was the purpose, or your intention, in doing this?', 'What does this say about what is important to you that you give value to?' or 'What were you hoping for?' could generate some interesting thoughts.

> It is important to me that I not be a victim and go along with things that bug me. I have a right to have a voice. I want to make sure he understands that being respected is really important to me. I hope that he will make more of an effort to be on time or recognize that I won't keep on waiting for him.

At this point it is important to move into a re-authoring conversation in order to position these preferences and skills in a story of the social and relational history of the development of these know-hows, and also to consider what might be made possible in the future, having become re-acquainted and re-familiarized with these preferences and skills. In attempting to thicken the storyline of the social and relational history of the skill, a possible starting question could be: 'You have made some comments about how important it is to you not to be a victim, and you have mentioned having to stand up against people before, so I wonder where, and how, you first began to think and behave that way?' Having moved into a re-authoring conversation, it is important to remember to ask the kinds of questions that would allow the person to focus on a series of events across time that thicken the storyline of being able to 'stand up against' people when necessary, by asking questions across time and within both the landscape of identity and the landscape of action, as described in Chapter 1.

Finally, it is important to remember that conversations make a difference and that it is useful to help the person think about what difference this conversation might make in the future, as most people attend professional services hoping for change. This can involve simply asking: 'What difference might it make if you hold on to these memories and commitments that you've been remembering and describing?'

> I have seen a lot of disrespect from my father to my mother, but I made a choice not to be like my mother in relationships. I have had to stand up to other people from time to time at work and I even left one job because of the disrespect I recognized in a supervisor. I respect others and I deserve to be respected. I will not be a door mat. I will stand up against disrespect when necessary.

In considering providing another case example to demonstrate the use of the absent but implicit conversation in practice, Hiedi,[1] a social worker who works as a member of a family health team in a small rural medical clinic, offered to provide a case description from her work. She has indicated that she has found the absent but implicit conversation extremely helpful in her practice.

There are limited counselling and mental health services available in the community in which I work for a family health team. I have therefore had a significant number of referrals from the family physicians for women over the age of 50 years who have been diagnosed with anxiety or depression. The women have often tried to meet with a psychiatrist and have been prescribed anti-depressants, but have noticed limited change in their moods and condition. When I initially meet with the majority of these women, they express significant frustration with the 'supports' they have received to date and they have preconceived notions of what they want from counselling. When discussing goals for counselling, they initially identify that they want to learn new skills (anger management or assertiveness skills) or to problem solve their situations (financial stress or dealing with conflicts with adult children). I initially attempted to provide women in these situations with the information they had requested using models they had become familiar with in previous counselling (solution-focused or cognitive behaviour therapy approaches and materials). The women would experience some initial relief or short-term change, but they often returned for the second or third session with the same complaint. I was concerned when they expressed further disappointment in themselves because they were unable to make the changes they had wanted and had seen this as a personal failure.

I began using the 'absent but implicit' conversation map to help shape discussions and gather details about the complaint and what the women were doing in response. I started to notice more meaningful discussions that seemed to enable women to make longer-term changes that significantly improved their overall moods. One woman I was working with particularly comes to mind to help illustrate this concept.

Betty was 62 years old and requested counselling to assist her with managing her anger and dealing with conflict with her grown-up children. She had been diagnosed with breast cancer, which had resulted in bilateral mastectomies. Betty had worked in the healthcare field and was retired at the time I began meeting with her. She said she was feeling that she was at a point in her life where she could enjoy her retirement, spend time with her grandchildren and volunteer in her community. However, her children had informed her that due to her anger, they no longer wanted to have contact with her and she would not be able to see her grandchildren unless she went to counselling and made some changes. Betty was very upset by this ultimatum and did not know how to respond. She had been married for over 40 years, and had three grown-up children and four grandchildren. She was aware that she could be 'difficult' at times, but was shocked that her children had presented her with his ultimatum. Her husband refused to attend counselling with her because he felt that they were not doing anything 'wrong'.

Step 1: Main gist of the complaint
Betty felt that she was 'being controlled' by her children. She described this as if her children were trying to become the 'alpha dogs' in her family. Her children would call to plan visits with the grandchildren, but also make what seemed to Betty to be unreasonable demands in order to facilitate visits.

Step 2: Name and describe the response to the complaint
Betty admitted she would, at times, become verbally aggressive with her children and would often decline their requests even if these were within her capabilities, so that they were aware that she could say 'no'. She said that this was her attempt to stand firm and stand up against what felt like their attempts to control her.

Step 3: Link to knowledge and skills

When asked if she had had this type of feeling before, Betty linked the feeling of her children trying to control her to when she was younger and she felt that her mother had also tried to control her. Betty resented her mother's attempts to control her and often fought her mother for independence.

I was curious about how Betty would describe how she had learnt to recognize 'being controlled' and how she had decided to take a stand against it. Betty said that she had learnt to 'stand up' to 'being controlled' when she was in college. She said that she had learnt about different ways of interacting with people through fellow students and especially when she met her husband. She learnt that trying to control others did not really work and that there were better options. She recalled learning different ideas as well as accessing resources and support to develop new skills that worked better in dealing with difficult situations.

Step 4: Justification

I asked Betty to think about what the purpose of standing up to being controlled was in her mind and what doing this implied was important to her. On reflection, Betty realized that the purpose of her 'standing up' against her perception of 'being controlled' by her children was her way of showing them that trying to control others 'doesn't work'. She wanted them to be able to learn this because she said that she cared about them and did not want them to make the same mistakes as she had made. Through further discussions, however, Betty came to the conclusion that she wanted to be more 'balanced' in her approach with her children in order to allow them to feel that they had 'some control' over situations, while at the same time allowing her not to feel like she was 'being controlled'.

The new awareness that Betty developed about her reactions to her complaint of not wanting to 'be controlled' by her children helped her see that at times she could be perceived as 'a difficult person' and that she did not always respond appropriately. She said that she needed to change some of her approaches to accomplish what was actually important to her. As Betty began to implement the changes that she intended, she noticed positive improvements in her relationships with her neighbours and close friends. Unfortunately, she suggested that she only noticed minor improvements in her relationships with her children. Nonetheless, Betty said she felt that she had made significant progress, because her reactions to her perceptions of 'being controlled' changed and as a result she noticed that her overall mood improved, her blood pressure lowered and she was able to sleep better at night.

I appreciate Hiedi's example of practice with the absent but implicit conversation, as it is a good reminder that shifts in attitudes and perceptions can come about and make a positive difference, and yet it is perhaps unrealistic to think that everything is going to improve drastically. If the people about whom someone is complaining (i.e. Betty's children) are not part of the conversation, it is useful to deconstruct the elements that are contributing to the complaint that can bring about some relief in the form of less anger and stress. The others' behaviours, however, are not necessarily going to change. In Betty's situation, her children's behaviours might slowly begin to change over time as they start to realize that Betty's changes have been maintained, but practitioners can only really work with the people directly involved in the conversation. If at some point Betty's children were interested in joining her in counselling sessions, externalizing conversations about the effects of conflict and control on their relationships could be interesting and useful.

Double listing in practice

Engaging in an absent but implicit conversation is only one way of putting into practice the notion of double listening. As suggested earlier in this chapter, a more fluid approach to double listening, which can be useful when there are no concerns about having to find ways to deconstruct complaints about other people, is listening for clues of alternative and preferred storylines and possibilities while also listening to descriptions of the problem storyline.

I had the privilege of reviewing a recording of an interview that Scot Cooper[2] conducted with a 17-year-old boy and his mother who attended a walk-in clinic. What was interesting to observe in Scot's session with Jake was that Scot put into practice the notion of double listening by asking frequently whether Jake believed that his behaviours and reactions were helping him move closer to, or further away from, his preferences. Scot clearly demonstrated the practice skill of listening for the problem storyline and alternative storyline at the same time. This is a good example of how the underlying principles of an absent but implicit conversation map, and the ideas of there being multiple storylines possible in someone's life, can be put into practice without having to use the structure of a map.

Jake's mum had brought him to the walk-in clinic because she was concerned about his drug use. He said that he realized his mother had concerns about his drug use, but he did not see it as much of a problem. In the post-session questionnaires, Jake indicated that he had found it beneficial to be able to talk to someone other than himself and that he was very hopeful that he could bring about change in his life. His mum indicated in her post-session questionnaire that she had realized through the session how much anger Jake was dealing with, and that she was hopeful that if he could continue with some ongoing sessions with someone to talk to about his anger, then he would be able to make some positive changes.

Since Jake and his mum provided consent for me to show the recording of their session for teaching purposes in my university classes, as well as for research and writing purposes, I have shown the initial stages of the interview to beginning social work students. They usually indicate surprise that Scot does not open the session by asking the mother and son what has brought them in for counselling, but rather starts by saying: 'No one likes to get introduced by their problems, I'm guessing, so we can come to your concerns in a little bit, but would it be okay if I got to know you a little bit away from the problem first? What are you into? What do you just love to do?'

This invitation has Jake start talking about the fact that he loves sport, and that he plays basketball and football. Scot demonstrates interest and curiosity and asks whether or not Jake plays on his school teams. This leads Jake to explain that he had played for the school football team, but he had decided to walk away because the team was 'crap'. Asking him more about this resulted in Jake explaining that he did not like the lack of sportsmanship on the team and the way he thought the coach favoured the older kids on the team whom he knew better, rather than encouraging the potential in the younger children who often showed more commitment to coming to practice regularly. Scot asks 'What rubs you the wrong way about this?', which is a nice example of a question that can assist someone in becoming clearer about their personal values and preferences. Jake then talks about the coach's behaviours as being unfair and Scot responds by asking whether fairness has always been important to him. This provides an example of being influenced by the notion of 'différance' that is contained within a word and the opportunities provided by thinking along the lines of absent but implicit and double listening conversations. Rather than being drawn into a conversation about unfairness, Scot realizes that Jake must know something about fairness if he is able to judge what is unfair. Jake responds to Scot's question by saying, 'Yeah, you treat me right and I'll treat you right.' Thinking in terms of a re-authoring conversation, and keeping in mind that a storyline about preferred ways of being will have a timeline, Scot asks: 'Has this been important to you for a long time? Where did you learn this from?' Jake says that he thinks it is just a mentality. As Scot is working from a framework that considers the social construction of both problems and preferences, he goes on to ask Jake's mother: 'Is this something you always wanted to teach him?' She smiles and agrees that it has always been important to her that he respect people, but she points out that sometimes he needs to learn how to manage his reactions when someone perhaps does not show him respect. Jake explains that if someone does not treat him right and it is only 'minor, dumb, I laugh, "ha" and walk away', but otherwise he says that he gets angry. Scot asks at this point, which is only seven minutes into the conversation, 'So does that get you closer to the kind of life you want or does it kind of bite you sometimes?' Jake says, 'It kind of bites me sometimes.'

These first seven minutes of a conversation with a narrative practitioner and teenage boy, who could very easily have been totalized by the presenting problem of 'drug use', demonstrate how it is possible to be curious about preferences and storylines and experiences that are separate from the problem storyline without avoiding the problem. By Scot's allowing the problem to arise through this broader curiosity in Jake's life, Jake and his mum were able to begin to develop a picture of how Jake experienced frustration and anger: these feelings often arose because of situations that he deemed unfair. They also became clearer about how Jake would try to relax by walking away, listening to music or perhaps smoking weed. Scot was able to ask, about each of those strategies, whether they brought Jake closer to his preferred life or further away. This provided Jake with a method of reflecting on, and developing, his personal agency in order to make thought-out decisions about how best to act in various contexts in order to move towards his preferred life. In fact, 30 minutes into the conversation Jake says, 'Well, when it comes down to it, I'm a pretty smart kid, if I apply myself, but the problem is I don't always apply myself.'

Jake appears remarkably open and willing to discuss his drug use and anger in his session with Scot, with no signs of defensiveness or denial. I think that this is very much as a result of Scot's therapeutic posture with him, which contributes to the kind of professional relationship where problems can be discussed in a manner that balances them with attempts to make changes. Nearer the end of the session, Scot also uses an externalizing conversation statement of position map 1 to deconstruct the effects of Jake's drug use on Jake, as well as on his mum and his siblings, which contributes further to Jake's growing sense of personal agency over his drug use.

The conversation between Scot, Jake and his mum also demonstrates the manner in which it is possible, within narrative practices, to move from one type of conversation (or conversation map) to another. Although I have presented the conversation maps as separate from one another in the first three chapters since it is easier to learn them as separate conversations with beginnings, middles and endings, in real practice situations there can be a greater sense of fluidity from one to another. I will describe the process of deciding when to use the various conversation maps and how they fit together in the bigger overall picture of therapeutic conversations in the following chapter.

Conclusion

I hope that the potential benefits of double listening and engaging in absent but implicit conversations have been clear in this chapter. I have found these approaches particularly useful when I would otherwise have become stuck and not known how to respond to concerns and complaints. It is a good reminder that as narrative practitioners it is possible to let go of some of the worries about wanting to be helpful and know how to respond to, and address, various concerns. By demonstrating a true curiosity about other people's descriptions, and tuning our ears to listen for 'différance', it is possible to assist people in both listening to their preferences and hopes, and reconnecting to a story of the development of skills in knowledge, which they might have previously minimized or disregarded. This narrative practice skill contains elements of sleuthing, or, as White has described it, 'investigative reporting' (White, 2007a, p. 27), as practitioners move beyond thin descriptions and become more fascinated by complexity and thick descriptions. As White points out, taking on this posture of curiosity seems to encourage people who are complaining also to assume a stance of investigative reporting, allowing them to develop skills in building a full exposé of the details of their situation and taking a stand about how to bring about change.

I agree with White, wishing that he had stressed this aspect of narrative practices earlier in his career. I wish he had had longer to reflect on this approach to responding to complaints, before it had to be taken up by his colleagues and friends. In my last training session with him, I and my fellow practitioners found the eight steps of the 'absent but implicit' conversation, as he had initially described it, difficult to integrate into our set of skills. Although I am hopeful that the four-step version of the map I have presented in this chapter might be slightly simpler to integrate, I think that what I find most difficult are the first two steps of the conversation. Developing a curiosity about the underlying gist of people's complaints, rather than becoming distracted by judging the behaviours of the person at the centre of the complaints, can be a challenge at times. Having then to ask the types of questions that assist people in reflecting on their complaints as actions, which indicate that they are resisting something being implied by the other person, is also a challenge. Thankfully, as I have pointed out in Chapters 1 and 2, these new skills simply take practice to integrate fully, and do become more smoothly woven into practice. Although I initially used the re-authoring conversation map to take notes on, I no longer need to do this to remind myself of the elements of re-authoring. I now rarely need to remind myself of the steps of the externalizing and re-membering conversations, and find that I have integrated the steps more smoothly into my practice. In beginning to learn the steps of the absent but implicit conversation, however, I needed to start from scratch and again required visual reminders of the steps. This conversation also becomes simpler over time if the underlying ideas are understood. It is then possible to be more creative with the wording of questions and better able to assist people in uncovering the values and skills that are contained within their complaints.

Notes

1. Hiedi, as did Diane who presented a case example for inclusion in Chapter 1, completed the narrative therapy elective I teach in the university graduate programme and since graduating has been continuing to meet in a narrative consulting group I facilitate.

2. Scot Cooper is a brief narrative practitioner/supervisor who works in south-western Ontario in Canada in a child and adolescent clinic. He also provides training in narrative therapy nationally and internationally through the Brief Narrative Practices Project.

4 Moving between the Conversation Maps

Introduction

As I have suggested in earlier chapters, despite having found it extremely useful to learn the steps of the conversation maps in order to begin practising narrative therapy, I am also aware that the maps can initially cause confusion and consternation in some people. Not only have some beginning narrative practitioners struggled with learning the conversation maps without feeling overly controlled by them, many have also expressed confusion about how the conversation maps might fit together in practice and flow from one to another. It has been in response to these types of questions that I have developed a meta map in order to provide an illustration of how the various conversation maps can fit together. It is also important to keep in mind what White (2007a) has suggested regarding the maps: 'that the boundaries are often blurred' (p. 250).

Russell and Carey (2004) suggest that there is no right or wrong way to approach a narrative conversation and no right or wrong element to externalize in an externalizing conversation.[1] Through conversations with people, various problems, skills and initiatives can be discovered and externalized in order for people to become clearer about their hopes and preferences. Each member of a family in a conversation may experience a situation differently and find benefits in externalizing different aspects, resulting in a fluid use of the externalizing conversations. As White (2007a) has also suggested, these conversation maps are intended to provide some signposts along the journey rather than to be prescriptive. It is possible to double back on a journey and take another route. The conversation maps are best used in a flexible manner, but, as I pointed out in Chapter 2, becoming comfortable enough to be fluid and flexible with the maps only comes with practice and experience; a little more assistance with structure is often useful when beginning to practise narratively.

In learning the conversation maps as separate maps for separate issues (re-authoring, the two externalizing maps, re-membering, and absent but implicit), students can experience a sense of choppiness. In addition, I have been asked how they should decide when to use which map and when to move from one map to another. In attempting to move away from centring the expertise of the therapist, and instead towards centring the expertise of the person who has requested, or been mandated for, services, it would be rather ironic and self-defeating to put the conversation maps into a position of power. They are only tools to assist in the process of centring the other person's expertise, preferences, hopes and values. The therapeutic posture, the quality of the helping relationship and the ability to be truly present and mindful with the person are all crucial in order to use the conversation maps in a useful rather than prescriptive manner.

Ruch, Turney and Ward (2010) provide a thorough and timely reminder of the importance of what is at the heart of practice: the relationship. Doel (in Ruch, Turney & Ward, 2010, pp. 199–200) reviews research that explores what people who have used services say about relationships, pointing out that they appreciate the following:

- Understanding the intentions and purposes of the worker *[being transparent and non-manipulative]*.
- Contributing to the work of the service *[honouring and respecting what people bring in the way of their own skills and expertise to the process]*.
- Receiving help speedily.
- The worker's ability to respond to feelings not always expressed *[a form of double listening]*.
- The worker's concern and attention, even if change is not possible.[2]
- The worker's ability to exercise care, even when exercising control *[another form of transparency regarding power and mandates, which can be perceived as less controlling and more respectful]*.

Doel goes on to say that he believes an unnecessary dichotomy has been set up between relationship-based social work and task-centred social work. He suggests that relationship-based work has become associated with psychodynamic work, which fell out of favour in social work circles and so lost its importance. He says that this would have been at a time when 'the notion of relationship became totemistic, an end in itself, and identified as something to be used to get at the "real problems"' (in Ruch, Turney & Ward, 2010, p. 206). Doel points out that the 'relationship' in relationship-based practice and the 'task' in task-centred work are both essential elements for social workers attempting to work effectively with people, and that it is hard to imagine social work without both a developing relationship and the performance of some kind of task. He says, 'What methods like task-centred social work have to offer is a *means* to develop the relationship between service user and social worker, then a structure by which that relationship can be employed to progress the work. This is sometimes referred to as a purposive relationship' (p. 207).

The use of narrative practice conversation maps can contribute to the development of the quality of the purposive relationship that people value and find respectful, while providing the structure to assist people in becoming re-acquainted with their skills, values, preferences and hopes. I agree with Ruch, Turney and Ward (2010) as they describe the importance of reflective practice and supervision in order to ensure the proper use of the relationship in relationship-based practice. In wishing to respond to the issues that are problematic within contemporary social work and the suggestions made in the Munro Review (Munro, 2011), it is not going to be useful to ignore the development of methods of practice and only focus on the quality of the relationship. It is going to be necessary to be careful and reflective about the effects of certain practice methods and thoughtful, therefore, about which methods to take up and incorporate into practice. Rather than falling into the debate about whether task or relationship is more important, it will be more effective for the people with whom we work if we develop skills in both areas.

I acknowledge that by developing and introducing yet another diagram as a meta map to assist with providing some idea of how the conversation maps fit together, I could be perceived as even more rigidly directing the course of conversations, but I am offering this meta map in the spirit of imaging when and how the conversation maps might flow one from another. Making decisions about when and if to move from one focus to another involves reflecting *in* practice about how and where conversations are going, as well as checking with the other people regarding how they are feeling about the direction of the conversation. In this way, the helping relationship and the people within that relationship are privileged over the structure of the map. I encourage readers to consider these ideas regarding a meta map framework in the spirit in which I have intended: with tentativeness and an openness to experiment with whether this is helpful or not.

When to use each conversation map

I will briefly review each of the conversation maps that I have described in the first three chapters in order for the description of the proposed meta map to be coherent.

The re-authoring conversation is used in order to generate thicker and more detailed descriptions of the problem storyline, which is made up of a series of events over time according to a plot or theme, with a richness added through the landscape of identity as well as the landscape of action. This is done in order to assist people in moving towards a preferred alternative storyline, which again will include a series of events in a landscape of action, linked over time according to a theme. The alternative storyline will also include values, preferences, hopes and dreams within the landscape of identity.

The externalizing conversation regarding the problem, the statement of position map 1, is most often used if the person receiving services has become totally identified by the problem or diagnosis, or has internalized a discourse that is having problematic effects: for instance, the romanticization of abusive behaviours (Béres, 1999, 2001). Common examples of this situation might include working with a child who has been totalized as ADHD; a person presenting as anxious; or someone labelled anorexic, a victim or an abuser.

As people begin to distance themselves from being totalized by a problem, recognizing that the problem is the problem rather than that they are the problem, they are able to examine the effects of the problem in their life and make judgements about those effects (White, 2007a). They are then asked what their judgements imply are important to them. Through these steps they will often begin to develop an initiative to counteract the problem, or will start to experiment with new skills. An example of this might involve people moving away from describing themselves as alcoholics (Béres, 2010) and, through examining the effects of alcohol in their lives, beginning to look instead at the role and effects of sobriety in their lives. Rather than merely assuming that any alternative to the problem will be a good thing, it is important to move through the steps of an externalizing conversation, the statement of position map 2, in regard to the new skill or initiative. This will allow people in this situation to look at the effects of sobriety (for example, improved relationships with children, but also a letting go of drinking friends, perhaps) and for them to judge whether these are the effects they would prefer. People make these judgements and link them to their own personal values and preferences, adding to their sense of agency and ability to follow through with intentions, rather than being trapped by a particular view of their identity.

A re-membering conversation is a powerfully moving conversation, especially when it concerns grief, allowing for the honouring of relationships with people who have had positive effects. Rather than suggesting a letting go and forgetting of people in order to move on, which is often a mainstream discourse about grief, the re-membering conversation puts into practice notions about the social construction of identity and celebrates the manner in which the person remembering, and the person who has died, have had an impact on one another's lives. This is also a productive conversation to have following an externalizing conversation about a new skill, since it can assist people in deciding who in their life might be best able to support them in their new skill or initiative. People who are attempting to limit the effects of alcohol in their lives and preferring to support a commitment to sobriety will probably need to elevate the significance of some people in their lives over others, for instance.

The absent but implicit conversation is used when people are complaining about another person or a situation and that person is not part of the conversation, as would be the case in providing couple or family counselling.

Since each of these conversation maps might be used with just one person or family over the course of several sessions, it is useful to think through how they all fit together within the bigger picture of the course of counselling or service provision. One map might take a few sessions to complete, a different problem might be externalized each week for a few weeks, or a different map might be used each week. It is, therefore, useful to think of the person's storylines within the re-authoring conversation map as the main aspect of the work, and then visualize how the other conversation maps fit together to support the movement from a problem storyline to alternative storylines.

The meta map

The beginning framework of the meta map is the re-authoring conversation map, since it provides a representation of a timeline from the remote past into the future, along with the two landscapes of storylines: the landscape of action and the landscape of identity.

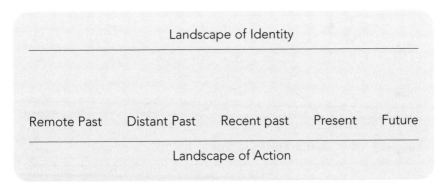

Figure 4.1 Re-authoring conversation map

Source: Adapted from White's 'Workshop Notes' posted on www.dulwichcentre.com.au

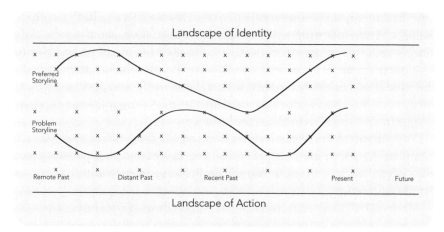

Figure 4.2 Events and storylines represented on a re-authoring conversation map

Imagining the vast number of events in a person's life that could be plotted on the re-authoring conversation map, it is possible to represent a smattering of these events across the timeline. Some of these events could be linked together to form the problem storyline, while others could form a preferred storyline. In representing two storylines on the timeline, it is useful to remember that each storyline has a landscape of action and a shared landscape of identity.

With both the problem storyline and a preferred storyline positioned on the re-authoring conversation map, it is possible to imagine that a problem that needs to be externalized, through the use of a statement of position map 1, is probably going to be associated with the problem storyline. An event

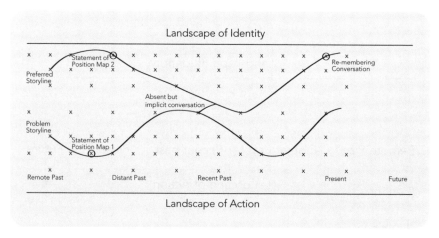

Figure 4.3 Meta map

that makes up part of an alternative or preferred storyline, on the other hand, is more apt to include skills and initiatives that could generate a statement of position map 2 externalizing conversation.

Events in a preferred storyline might also involve people who could be elevated in importance through a re-membering conversation, moving, therefore, from a re-authoring conversation to a re-membering conversation. It is also possible that, through discussing memories of someone who has been important, a re-membering conversation could be used in order to support a new skill that is part of a preferred storyline: moving, in this case, from a re-membering conversation to a conversation about the preferred storyline.

An absent but implicit conversation can be imagined as occurring as a bridge from a problem storyline to a preferred storyline, since this conversation incorporates notions of double listening: hearing what is valued and what is precious while also listening to complaints about other people and situations. These conversations often begin with elements of a problem storyline, but open up discussions of preferences, knowledge and skills that are aspects of preferred storylines.

Practice examples

Gillian was referred to me because she was struggling with still feeling angry about the emotional abuse she had experienced from her former husband. She indicated, as she was setting up her initial appointment, that his drug use and resulting bankruptcy had affected her so that she now felt she was having difficulty trusting people.

When we first met, I asked her to introduce herself as separate from the problems she wanted to discuss. Particularly, I asked her how she had been managing, and who and what she had been finding supportive, during the time she had been dealing with the consequences of her marriage. I expressed curiosity regarding how she had been coping while she had been thinking about initiating counselling. It is useful to engage people in these types of reflections in order to highlight any naturally occurring supports. This acts as a reminder that, as painful memories are stirred up, there are people and activities that have previously been helpful and could probably be helpful again. This assists in de-centring the therapist, and ensures that people do not become overly reliant on the therapist, since it clarifies that there are some natural supports that can also be helpful. Asking Gillian these questions set the stage for the broader re-authoring conversation, as she described some people and events over time that had provided her with support.

Since a timeline is an element of both the problem storyline and the preferred storyline, this process moved us slowly on to the re-authoring conversation map. Gillian spoke about her mother and friends as great supports. She talked about enjoying her job and her colleagues and also enjoying her exercise classes at the local gym. She soon began to move into the problem storyline, however, and described the events that made up the storyline of her marriage, and also events within the story of her current relationship. She talked about being frustrated with how easy-going her current partner was. She said that she was also frustrated with herself because she was not proud of how easily she could slip into nagging him. She said that, although she wished he had more ambition, she also wished she was not so bothered by this. She explained that she did not like herself when she engaged in these behaviours that she called 'nagging'. By this point in the first conversation Gillian had touched on two separate, but related, relationship problem storylines. She had considered her husband driven and successful in the early stages of their relationship and, although she realized that this was not perhaps a full description of what he had been like, since during this time he also developed a serious drug addiction, she said that she felt caught up in wanting something similar to those beginning stages again. She also realized that she had been deceived by her husband and so she thought there was the chance she should not trust anyone else in a relationship again. She was providing hints about her preferences – hard work and ambition – but since she clearly said that she did not like being a nag, I asked her how she would prefer to be in order to open up the possibility for discussions about a preferred storyline. She said that she wanted to be in a healthy relationship in which both she and her partner worked hard and saved money. She wanted to be healthy herself and to continue to be active at her gym so that she felt physically healthy as well as emotionally balanced.

I rarely suggest 'homework' to people for between appointments, because when I worked from more of a cognitive behaviour therapy approach I found that if people were not motivated to complete homework, they could present as feeling like failures for not having done the work. Gillian, on the other hand, asked for some tasks to complete before returning; given her drive and focus on hard work, this was consistent with her preferences. I suggested that if she wanted to keep a journal during the week, she might like to reflect on what her preferences implied that she privileged and valued. I explained that becoming clearer about personal values often helps people make decisions about how they want to manage situations in their lives.

Gillian returned for a follow-up appointment and read segments of her journal. She talked about her anger towards her partner. She also said that she thought she would rather not be in a relationship that involved her having to put up with someone who she thought was not right for her. On the other hand, she also talked about wanting to cultivate more of an attitude of 'let it be'. These insights provided material for both a statement of position map 1, as we externalized anger, and a statement of position map 2, as we externalized 'let it be'.

In a later session, Gillian began to think that her focus on work, and needing to achieve certain goals in life, was perhaps undermining her preference for 'let it be'. She realized that working hard was very important to her so she was not going to stop taking pride in her accomplishments, but she wanted to integrate more of a 'go with the flow' attitude both inside and outside of her work life. She thought that she might have more fun this way and not take things so seriously all the time. She said that she thought this meant, for her, that she should try to cultivate a greater ability to be spontaneous and to respond to spur-of-the-moment invitations when she received them, with an open mind. By asking her who would be least surprised to hear her making these commitments to these types of changes in her life, she indicated that a friend of hers, Rose, would be least surprised. This provided an opportunity to engage in a re-membering conversation, which supported her movement towards her preferred storyline. It also bolstered her social network and the social construction of her 'go with the flow' identity.

Gillian and I only met for six sessions, moving from the re-authoring conversation to the externalizing conversations and on to the re-membering conversation. The later conversations contributed to thickening the storylines that had been sketched out in the first session. By the time we were talking in the last two sessions, Gillian had already developed a clear sense of what was most important to her and some ideas about how to continue moving in those preferred directions.

The complexity of a person's situation will obviously affect the length of time that might be required for any one of the conversation maps. I have found that, in some situations, I have taken a whole hour-long session to talk with someone who is describing the characteristics of a problem to be externalized, and we might only finish that one step of a conversation in that first session. Each map does not need to be completed in one session and, in fact, the maps are not particularly useful if rushed through. I have discovered that I need to remind students of the benefits of a slower pace when learning these conversations: it isn't a race. A true sense of curiosity, and a willingness to linger and loiter in the maps, helps develop the thick descriptions that support movement into preferred ways of being.

In a walk-in clinic setting, as in the example of Scot's work with Jake in Chapter 3, it is possible to move through a couple of different conversation maps in just the one session. Yet, at the other end of the continuum, when I was in an agency where I worked primarily with adult survivors of sexual abuse, some people attended counselling for a year or more. During that time, I might have spent several months moving back and forth between the landscape of action and the landscape of identity in the problem storyline, as someone slowly broke the silence of her experiences and began to give voice to the pain inherent in the problem storyline. During that process, however, she might also remember positive experiences that were separate from her experiences of abuse and an alternative storyline would begin to develop so that she could begin to see that there was more to her life, and could continue to be more to her life, than merely abuse. Practical issues would need to be dealt with from time to time also, such as providing support letters for applications for housing. At other times, I wrote letters of support for victim's compensation.

I probably worked with Jane for longer than anyone else. She talked about having been sexually abused by her father multiple times. She explained that she had been removed from the home, but then returned to her mother who told her it was Jane's fault that her father was in prison. She described further forms of emotional, physical and sexual abuse from other extended family members during her childhood; when her father was released from prison and reunited with Jane's mother, Jane moved away from home as a teen. She also described three consecutive abusive relationships with men as an adult. After she had talked about the problem storyline of abuse and had begun to experience anger about her experiences and their effects, she slowly moved into an alternative storyline in which she began to realize that she wanted justice in the form of compensation. From time to time, we were able to externalize an emotion or behaviour that she did not like, and also externalize, and support the development of, new skills. She demonstrated a great deal of resilience and love of life. Rather than learning not to trust people, she began to reach out and develop new friendships and interests. When she was awarded a fairly significant amount of money as compensation through the victim's compensation process, she moved away to a rural community where the money was sufficient as a down-payment on a small house and she started life afresh. She gave me a small piece of slate on which she had painted a mountain and waterfall scene as a going-away and thank-you gift. Her sense of her identity had moved from 'victim' to 'survivor' to 'artist' and 'new friend to many' in her new community.

Another practice example is presented in Chapter 7 and provides a description of working with a young woman with refugee status, assisting her in the process of applying for permanent residency and finding a method of integrating into a new country. In her situation, a great deal of time was initially spent in the conversations about the problem storyline in order fully to document her reasons for needing refuge, before integrating other conversations.

Conclusion

The meta map that I have developed and described in this chapter has been designed as an overall picture of the way in which the conversation maps can be visualized as fitting together and supporting the commitments of narrative practice. I have presented this meta map within the context of the issues that I reviewed in Chapter 1 about the importance of the ethics, politics and philosophy of narrative practice. What is most important is to develop the kind of relationships with people in which their skills and knowledge are privileged and supported and they are able to become clearer about their hopes, dreams and preferences. Each conversation map focuses in on a small area within the larger process of narrative practice. I think that it is useful to visualize the maps in the overall context, so that they do not become ends in themselves, but are rather the means by which a person can accomplish the preferred changes. I have shared this meta map with former students, who have given feedback that it has helped them begin to gain a better understanding of when, and why, to use the various conversation maps. I am hoping that others might find it helpful in a similar manner.

I have also described in this chapter the way in which the movement between maps might occur in a walk-in clinic, or over the course of more than a year of appointments. I have shown how the maps can be integrated into practice alongside the need also to write letters and provide more pragmatic types of service and case management. Keeping in mind this bigger picture of storylines of events and conversation maps will, perhaps, assist new narrative practitioners in remembering that it is possible to hold on to the overall framework and attitudes of narrative practices and move in and out of the conversation maps as time and opportunity become available.

Notes

1. Russell and Carey's chapter regarding externalizing conversations is also posted on the Dulwich Centre's website at http://www.dulwichcentre.com.au/externalising.html.

2. Denis Costello, a former clinical supervisor, used to say that just like Simon of Cyrene helped carry Jesus's cross in the story of the crucifixion in St Mark's gospel in the Christian Bible (chapter 15, verse 21), he believed that in our practice we are sometimes called just to help people carry their burdens, when change is not possible. This attitude also shares something in common with Buddhist approaches to suffering and non-attachment. Sometimes it is struggling against suffering that can bring about more suffering, whereas a sense of non-attachment to outcome can bring a sense of relief. It appears as though 'clients' also report valuing this type of support.

PART

II

The Narrative Approach in Context

A Narrative Approach to Agency Practice: Note Taking, Assessment Writing and Consultation

Introduction

It has been important to me to attempt to develop methods of practice that are consistent with my personal and professional values and worldview, moving towards congruence between my direct practice methods and my conduct in agency-based interactions and teaching. This may sound simple and straightforward. What I have found, however, is that just as people learning narrative skills in direct practice may find that they need to let go of some of their other ways of working to develop narrative interactions fully, it is necessary to reflect on the taken-for-granted approaches to note taking, assessment writing and working with colleagues and students. This is in order to be able to consider more thoughtfully the politics and assumptions underlying mainstream methods of writing and consulting, for instance, and to make choices about how otherwise to write, supervise or teach so that we do not totalize or pathologize people, or privilege our expertise over others' experiences.

As I have suggested in Chapter 1, narrative practices have been influenced and shaped by post-structuralist and post-modern philosophy. In Béres, Bowles and Fook (2011), we discuss the common underlying theories that critical reflection of practice, narrative therapy and cultural studies share. We suggest that post-structuralist and post-modern philosophy and theories that point out the power of language in creating our understandings and engagement with the world are two of the main influences shared by these areas of practice and inquiry. Chang (2010), in describing narrative therapy as one of a handful of post-modern therapies, also suggests that what makes a post-modern therapy post-modern is partly the move away from 'a modernist view of language in which language is presumed to represent or symbolize internal mental constructs' (p. 20) to a post-modern 'view of language, in which language constitutes or constructs social reality, as persons interact with one another' (p. 20).

We particularly draw on the work of Derrida, Foucault, Deleuze and Parnet in describing the circulation of language in narrative practice in

Innovations in Narrative Therapy (Duvall & Béres, 2011). We describe the vulnerability and tentativeness of language, the need to be intentional and creative in the use of language, and we also suggest the privileging of the voices, meaning and stories of those who come to be engaged in narrative practices. It was within this context that I was interested to learn of Deleuze and Parnet's (2002) horror in reviewing transcripts and accounts of psychoanalytic sessions where they saw the psychoanalyst interpreting and moving so far away from what was actually said by the child as to imply a forcing of what was being said into the psychoanalyst's ways of categorizing. This forcing is not consistent with narrative ways of working, nor with many of the current psychoanalytically influenced ways of working, which would encourage a privileging of the other person's meaning-making. Nonetheless, I believe that it would be disingenuous to discount our own meaning-making and ways of viewing the world as narrative practitioners engaged in witnessing and perhaps recounting others' stories in our note taking and written assessments. A narrative approach does not involve abdicating power or knowledge, but rather acknowledging others' skills and knowledge and being transparent and tentative about our own reactions, thoughts and judgements. In using 'I' in written recording, it becomes clearer that we cannot be a totally objective and disinterested writer. We are subjective, but professionally subjective, as we bring our training and our expertise to our engagement with people and to our writing. I believe that it is most ethical to be clear about how we are reacting to circumstances and what our assessments are based on, in order for others, who may have access to the documentation, to be able to form their own reactions. There is not only one true and accurate way of looking at someone's life, and this should be made clear in how we write about people in our work.

Hibel and Polanco (2010), in describing the process of assisting students to learn how to 'tune the ear' for listening in narrative therapy, suggest the need to begin to reflect, for instance, on what it is we may have tuned into and heard in a conversation, and why it is that we selected those particular statements as more significant over other statements. They encourage and support the development of skills in 'listening *to*' rather than 'listening *for*'. Listening *for* implies listening only for those statements that trigger an 'aha', and the chance to categorize or label based on what is already known. Listening *to*, on the other hand, suggests an open curiosity where 'there are no single truths to be uncovered. Consistent with Bateson's ... ideas about the multiplicity of "facts" imminent in any perception and White's attention to double listening ..., instead there are multiple threads of meaning available to be inquired about and explored' (Hibel & Polanco, 2010, p. 55). I would add, however, that in order to learn how to assist people in moving towards preferred storylines, it is important to start listening *for* possibilities.

A commitment to double listening, for instance, requires training the ear to listen for stories within stories and traces of preferences within complaints. The difference within this narrative context of listening *for* is that therapists do not judge the significance of these possibilities, but rather ask the people engaged in the conversation with them to consider the implications. This process has been fully described in Chapter 3.

Note taking

It is not unusual for social workers, therapists or counsellors to worry about whether note taking in a meeting might set up an unnecessary boundary between themselves and the people engaged in services with them. Although they might think that they need to take notes in order to remember important details, they may be concerned that the taking of notes in session can contribute to the impression that the professional is the expert in the exchange. Despite these concerns, it is possible to take notes in a manner that privileges other people's knowledge and authority in their life, which would be consistent with the philosophy and politics of narrative therapy.

In a narrative therapy course that I teach, I present part of a digital video recording of a training session that Michael White facilitated for the American Association for Marriage and Family Therapy in 1992, to show how Michael described his work. In this recording he presents clips from videotaped sessions. He shows and discusses his work with Chris, whom he describes as someone with a long psychiatric career, who had received a diagnosis of manic depressive illness. Michael draws attention to how he is taking notes, which often initially unsettles students, offering a clear alternative for how to take notes in such a way as to shine the light on the other person's expertise and knowledge. Michael takes notes fairly constantly throughout the session and explains that he does this in order to record Chris's movement into a position of authority on his own life. He says that he acts as a scribe and is able to refer back to how Chris has phrased his thoughts and ideas, in previous sessions and earlier on in the current session. After years of experience as a patient in psychiatric institutions, this is a new experience for Chris. At one point he asks Michael if he has any information that he thinks would help. Michael explains that he does not take up the invitation to become the authority, but rather says that maybe he will have some ideas later on in the discussion if he could ask a few more questions. As Chris moves back into reflecting on, and answering further questions about, what he thinks about his situation and his reactions, Michael is able to continue bolstering Chris's confidence in his own meaning-making, ideas and knowledge of himself.

People who have had prior experience of being 'clients' or 'patients' may expect counsellors to be guided by checklists, or the need to gather specific information for a written assessment, and expect note taking to ease the written requirements of the job. People may expect counsellors to ask specific questions and listen *for* themes that help to make a diagnosis or to complete a written recording. I therefore explain to people in initial sessions that I would like to take notes to help me remember the details they tell me. I tell them that I will only be jotting down how they say things and will not be writing down my observations or thoughts. That allows me to refer back to my notes and use the same language that the other person has used, to privilege the other person's way of putting ideas and support that person in further developing confidence in the ability to name and describe experiences and make meaning of them.

In the last few years that I was working in full-time direct practice, I facilitated narrative therapy groups for men who had used abusive behaviours. The development of my narrative practice in this area was influenced by White's friend and colleague Allan Jenkins (1990), as well as by Fisher and Augusta-Scott (2003). I was particularly interested in Fisher's (2005) creativity in regard to the use of note taking in group settings, and also in his individual practice with men who had used abuse in intimate relationships.

Fisher suggests that he often documents lists of ideas that the men develop by writing their ideas on white boards, or on flip charts as I did with my group co-facilitator, during the group discussions. My co-facilitator and I would type up the lists prior to the next session and distribute the men's words back to them in a more legible format. Fisher, however, became more creative and would use a Polaroid-style camera to photograph what he had written on the white boards; he is probably using a digital camera now. The Polaroid pictures he took could then be given to the men or put into their files. He also indicated that he had begun to use white boards in individual sessions with the men, rather than taking notes on a pad of paper. He explained that he would draw four quadrants on a white board and use each of the quadrants for one section of an externalizing conversation,[1] taking notes in the relevant section of the diagram as a man spoke about, for instance, the characterization of the abuse, the effects of the abuse, the evaluation of the effects, and his justification for why he had evaluated the effects in that manner. In this way the man in the conversation with Fisher could see the notes clearly as they were written, keeping the note-taking process visible and transparent. Fisher indicated that he would also photograph these notes and descriptions, thereby being able to use them as part of the recording. He indicated that there usually was no identifying information on these photographs and often the men gave consent to have the photographs of their externalizing conversations also put on the wall in the waiting room, so that men coming to the agency could see how others had examined their own behaviours. Fisher indicated that this appeared to contribute to the development of a context for men to be willing to discuss openly their struggles with abuse, and their struggles with the process of learning new ways of behaving, since they could see that other men were also willing to struggle with these issues.

Therapeutic documents

In their early work, White and Epston (1990) had already begun to develop their practice of providing documents to people in order to summarize, support and celebrate the developments that were occurring. In order to do this, they suggested the practice of writing letters to people, developing lists of ideas generated by people in session and providing certificates of achievement. Children appeared especially to enjoy receiving certificates that they could show to others. Photographs and photocopies of notes can also be considered a form of therapeutic document that could be appropriate as a reminder of conversations and learning.

Epston's (2012) work has continued to expand his approach in this area of therapeutic documents and written conversation, as he has developed carefully thought-out ways of using email with people, asking the sorts of questions that assist people in considering the social construction of both their problems and alternative ways of living. Although some agencies and practice settings might have guidelines limiting communication with 'service users' via email, letters can be mailed, or handed to people, if this possibility is discussed with them ahead of time and they are not concerned that the letters might end up in the wrong hands. Some practitioners, despite the usefulness of this approach, have indicated a concern about how time-consuming it can be to craft a letter carefully, and therefore conclude that they do not have the time for this. As White and Epston (1990) have suggested, however, these therapeutic letters can have much more significance for people than several more sessions, since they do clearly summarize and reinforce the insights and changes that have been coming about in a way that a further session sometimes does not. People are also able to keep the documents and re-read them at any time as a reminder of the changes and commitments made.

Speedy (2005) has developed a creative alternative to letters as therapeutic documents, suggesting that poetry can be written based on the words used in session. She draws on similar ideas to Bird's (2008) about listening for 'talk that sings'. I am especially careful to jot down words and phrases that people use that seem to 'sing' or 'sparkle', or that will 'jump off the page' as I review my notes. This provides a lovely use of the notes when they are truly only made up of the words and phrases the person has used in the conversation. In fact, I have found that it is much faster to craft a poem from the words used in session in the last few minutes of a meeting so that I can then give people a poem made of their words as they leave, rather than having to find the time to write it between appointments. I do not incorporate this into my practice all the time, but have found that people very much appreciate it when I have. I was also interested to hear from a former graduate student that she found this practice appreciated by adolescent boys with whom she was meeting due to their involvement in the criminal justice system. As I have not worked with this age group of boys very much, I would have erroneously thought that they might have considered poems ridiculous. What the social worker found, however, as she incorporated this practice into her work was that the boys were very proud of their ability actually to have said the words and phrases she highlighted and gave back to them in the form of poetry. They appeared to see that their poetry was similar to lyrics in songs or raps, which did interest them greatly.

In writing a poem it may be necessary to remove any type of internalized critic, since the poems do not need to be finely crafted and polished; rather, what is more important is that they are primarily made up of the exact words and phrases the person used. Linking these words and phrases into a poem merely requires creating the shape of a poem, while maintaining a focus on the purpose: to highlight new insights about values and movements towards preferences, despite the problems in the person's life. When I have practised this approach to generating therapeutic documents with students, I usually find that some students initially panic because they think they are unable to write poetry. Once they have taken a chance and created a poem based on the other person's words and have received feedback from that other person as to how meaningful it was to have been so clearly listened to and understood, the majority of students begin to realize how very useful this can be.

I wrote the following poem in a workshop that Mandy Pentecost and Jane Speedy (2006) facilitated in which people interviewed one another about their interests in narrative practice and then wrote one another poems based on the words used in the interview. This was for Pat, using only the words she had spoken:

Dreaming of …
Opening up spaces
for 'other than' conversations.
Spaces
for new stories
Spaces
for actively summarizing alternatives.

Dreaming of …
Changing the work setting
Offering new ways to explore
Moving beyond limitations and either/ors
Personally inspiring with dreams.

Speedy quotes Bachelard as having said, 'The great function of poetry is to give us back the statement of our dreams' (Speedy, 2005, p. 283). This is a form of double listening by which, rather than listening for material on which to base an assessment in the framework of a particular theory, the practitioner listens *to*, and *for*, people's hopes and dreams. White has commented on the benefits of 'exoticizing the domestic' (2004) and the act of shaping people's words into a poem is a simple method of integrating this notion into practice. Pentecost and Speedy point out that giving back a person's words in the form of a poem highlights the extraordinariness of the things that the person expressed. Speedy mentioned in the workshop that she has also written poems to psychiatrists in the United Kingdom when they have requested information regarding a patient. She said that they have responded favourably, but I have not yet taken that step.

Assessments and recording

When I last met with David Epston in a training and consultation context in October 2012, he asked me about the structure and focus of this book that I was in the process of writing at the time. I mentioned that I hoped to include in this particular chapter the challenges of attempting to work congruently with narrative practices when working in an agency setting. He immediately suggested that I consider visiting Walter Bera, founder and director of the Kenwood Therapy Center, LLC (typically called the Kenwood Center) in Minneapolis.[2] Epston said that he thought the Kenwood Center an excellent example of an agency that is infused with narrative practice principles in its direct practice, team consultations, training and inquiry. I therefore contacted Walter Bera and asked if I might visit and sit in on some of the meetings in order to be able to describe a centre that offers an example of how to operate narratively within all its practices. He and his partner, Jane Carlson, very kindly hosted me as a guest and I was able to sit in as an 'outsider witness' on one of his counselling sessions, for which consent had been provided by the person involved in the session, and in one of the team consultation meetings. He explained the process of maintaining files and provided me with a tour of the centre. It is unlikely that many narrative practitioners will have the chance to work in a setting that is organized like the Kenwood Center, where narrative ideas influence each of the aspects of the setting, but its practices may offer some examples that can be integrated into work in other contexts.

At the end of a full day at the Kenwood Center, Walter asked me about my reactions. The first thing that came to mind was the welcoming atmosphere and the 'feel' of the place. It seemed to me that much of the 'feel' is initially created by the use of Jane Carlson's photography, which is framed and hanging in the hallways. There are artefacts that have been created through collaborative practices, and gathered from travels, hanging in stairwells and offices, which all contribute to the sensation of walking into a well-loved and taken-care-of space, into which people can truly be welcomed and made to feel comfortable.

In reflecting back on my visit, I think another important aspect of the centre that contributes to its collaborative and respectful nature is the attitude that Walter and the other practitioners and staff demonstrate through their interactions with one another, which I also witnessed in Walter's interactions in the counselling session I observed. Respect was shown for each person, whether in the position of office staff, therapist-in-training, person requesting services or experienced practitioner. They appeared to put into practice a genuine curiosity about one another and respect for each other's thoughts and reflections.

It was particularly interesting to see how the Kenwood Center manages demands for written assessments and the maintenance of files. Walter generously shared the forms it uses and explained that the funders of its services, who are primarily third-party insurance companies in this context in the United States, have been completely satisfied to receive photocopies of the intake and progress questionnaires, assessment form and notes taken during sessions, as documentation of the services provided. He explained that the centre's practice is to review notes with people at the end of each session; to invite those people to sign the notes, along with the narrative practitioner; and then to provide photocopies of the notes to those same people. This keeps the process transparent and results in people not needing to wonder what else might be written about them. Walter described thinking of Madigan's question 'Who has the storytelling rights of the story being told? (Madigan, 2011, p. 9), as he explained this process of inviting the people with primary authorship of their stories to review and sign the recording regarding those stories.

Walter noted that preliminary research, which has included feedback from people receiving services, has supported the narrative-informed forms for therapeutic, quality assurance, supervision, training and research purposes (Bera, 2013a). He said that the centre uses the two-page Narrative Individual Family Questionnaire (NIFQ) 1 at intake and the NIFQ 2 at approximately two months into services as a progress assessment and then as a post-evaluation.[3] He went on to say that quantitative data and practitioner experience show significant change based on single-subject research design formats and group pre/post-design studies (Bera, 2013a). He explained that the centre also includes NIFQs in consultation meetings, and for training purposes, as a method of bringing the voices of people engaged in services into the meetings.

Walter provided a copy of the Kenwood Center Informed Consent and Narrative Therapy and Consultation Information form,[4] which is provided to people as they commence services in order to explain the approach used at the centre. Finally, he also provided a copy of the Individual Family Societal Narrative History, Evaluation, Assessment, Values and Plan[5] that is used at the Kenwood Center in place of a traditional 'diagnostic assessment'. He explained that he based these forms on the conversation maps, incorporating such questions as: 'Why are you committed to changing your life and relationships now?'; 'What values, hopes, dreams and visions of life, that you hold precious, are motivating you?'; and 'Can you tell me a story about these ideas and people that may have influenced you?' This last form integrates the traditional assessment concerns that might need to be included in many agency settings, but has incorporated narrative practice and participants' preferred ideas into the process. It is assumed that this assessment is completed with the person who has requested services and, therefore, it can provide a structure for asking about the problems and preferred solutions in a narrative framework. Walter Bera's Narragram™ (2013b) is part of the assessment form, providing a diagram, or structure, for visualizing the many aspects of a person's situation from a narrative perspective. Walter also explained to me that he develops the narragram[6] in session with people, drawing it on a flip chart and inviting people to express their thoughts and opinions about the effects of the problem, and other people involved, as they create this visual representation together. Just as Art Fisher photographs the notes he develops on white boards, Walter indicated that he also photographs the narragram that takes shape on the flip chart and includes the photograph in the person's file.

I have previously described some ideas about how to write about people respectfully from a narrative perspective in assessments (in Duvall & Béres, 2011). These are ideas that I also review with social work students beginning their professional careers. The ideas are informed by strength-based perspectives (Saleebey, 2009) and post-modern narrative approaches, and they result in written records that also meet the requirements set by regulatory bodies of professional practitioners and are clear and appropriate should they be subpoenaed to court. It is important, in other words, to maintain a recording. Most practitioners are most likely only to keep the informal notes until the formal recording is complete and then shred those informal notes. At the Kenwood Center, however, all notes are kept and signed. In either situation it is best to inform people of your recording-keeping practices. I think it is most ethical and respectful to keep in mind that records can be subpoenaed, so this limit to confidentiality needs to be explained ahead of time to people; and also that people may wish to look at their files, which can influence how you explain their situations. If people are contributing to the construction of their written assessments, this is less of a concern. It is important to be clear about how you know what you are reporting (e.g. you observed it, read about it in previous files or the person told you) and also the reason why you think what you think, if you have included those thoughts in the assessment. For example, rather than writing, 'Sylvia Jones is a 35-year-old single mother of three children, living in subsidized housing. She is an alcoholic and unable to care appropriately for her children', it is more transparent and respectful to move away from pathologizing and totalizing accounts and to write, 'Sylvia Jones reports that she is currently 35 years of age and that she is raising her three children as a single mother. I have visited her in her home, which is in a subsidized housing unit. She has admitted that she has been struggling with trying to control the effects of her overuse of alcohol and I am, therefore, concerned about her ability to consistently care appropriately for her children.' This form of writing does not avoid any problems and concerns the professional practitioner may have, but makes clear what the concerns are based on, and that some of what is reported is based on what the other person has said rather than on independent investigation and checking of facts. The recording should go on to include the mutually agreed goals, integrating the person's hopes and preferences. It is helpful to include descriptions of efforts that the person may have already attempted and an exploration of strengths such as spirituality, resilience and support systems that are available for ongoing efforts.

Team meetings and supervision

Supervision and team meetings, just like recordings, can sometimes seem like unwelcome demands on time, unless they are structured in such a way as to be supportive of the further development of practice skills. Some of the tasks associated with supervision and meetings may simply be in regard to administrative details, but the best aspects are those that support critical reflection of practice and the development of best practice through collaborative conversations.

The structure of an outsider witnessing conversation map, which can be used in community practice and within some clinical settings, can also be helpful as a non-directive approach for highlighting and reflecting on practice. Using the structure of an outsider witnessing conversation provides a method of making connections between people's practices, rather than setting up the types of conversations where people slip into criticism or advice-giving based on what they would have done in the same situation.

When using an outsider witnessing conversation one person, or a few people, is asked to listen in silence to the conversation going on between the others in the meeting. One practitioner might be describing work with a particular person, including some successful interactions and challenges experienced in attempting to move away from negative and pathologizing thinking about that person. Some of the team members might be asking questions for more clarification and some will sit silently as 'outsider witnesses' to the conversation. When the practitioner indicates feeling that everything relevant to the situation has been described, the outsider witnesses, if they are already familiar with the structure of the conversation map, can describe their responses; or if they are new to this practice, they can be interviewed using the steps involved in the outsider witnessing conversation map.

Example from a narrative consultation meeting

Just as in the conversation maps described in Chapters 2 and 3, this conversation map involves four areas of inquiry to assist with facilitating a movement from what is known and familiar, at the bottom of the 'map', to what is possible to know, at the top of the 'map'. I will describe how my colleagues and I recently used this structure in a narrative consultation meeting.

There are usually four stages within a meeting when this type of conversational framework is being used. The first stage involves a conversation between an interviewer and the person wanting consultation on a particular situation. The second stage involves a witness to the conversation discussing, or being interviewed about, the four areas of the outsider witnessing conversation. The third involves using the structure of the outsider witnessing conversation for a second time in order to interview the first person about what was interesting in what the witness described. The last stage involves a discussion between and among everyone involved in the process about what they will be taking away from the overall conversation.

Hiedi, Diane, Sandy and I met in a small narrative consultation group recently and we all agreed to use the framework of an outsider witnessing conversation for our consultation that evening. We do not always use this framework; sometimes we practise other conversation maps together when no one has a particular situation that she wants to discuss. This was a smaller group than usual, due to the Canadian winter with difficult driving conditions that evening and other demands on people's time. This framework, however, would also be useful in larger groups. What was important to keep in mind, which was confusing at times, was that the focus of the conversation was to be Hiedi's practice rather than the person with whom she was working. This can be a challenge when so much of consultation and supervision can inadvertently slip into more traditional frameworks of assessing the development of problems in people, rather than supporting the development of the practice skills that can assist people in moving beyond those problems.

Hiedi asked to discuss her ongoing work with Kim because she said she was worried that she could be doing more to support Kim in her wishes to make some changes in her life. She said that Kim had been referred to her within a family health clinic setting. Kim had been experiencing the effects of anxiety in her life and this had escalated to a point where her husband had taken her to the emergency ward of the local hospital. Hiedi explained that Kim did not want to take anti-anxiety medication and was requesting assistance in figuring out how to manage her anxiety better.

Hiedi had engaged Kim in an externalizing conversation about the effects of anxiety and through this process Kim had said that she wanted to make things normal. Hiedi reported that Kim also called herself a perfectionist and anxious during weeks when her husband, Philip, was away for work, but that she felt better and not alone with her thoughts when Philip was home.

Hiedi continued to give more of the background information to Kim's situation, saying that although Kim had said she had not been abused prior to leaving home at the age of 16, Philip had pointed out that Kim's home life had involved knife fights between siblings, which he thought could be described as abusive. Hiedi also said that Kim acknowledged this and then was able to point out that her first boyfriend, after she moved away from home, was involved in illegal activities, and that she had been relieved to meet her current husband, who was 'normal'. Hiedi said she had become interested in Kim's use of the word 'normal' and had asked her more about this. Kim had suggested that she had always been seeking 'normal' in her life, but that her normal had always been different. As an example, she said that her group of friends in school had been a mix of different types of people: none 'normal, but different normal'.

Hiedi went on to describe attempting an absent but implicit conversation about 'perfectionism', since Kim had been complaining about her perfectionism. Through our consultation Hiedi began to realize that the absent but implicit conversation was probably not the best conversation map to use for this, but that another externalizing conversation, this time about perfectionism, might have been more helpful. Nonetheless, she said that she had asked Kim what she was standing up against when she complained about, and tried to resist, perfectionism. She also said that Kim explained how, as she had started to stand up against too many demands from others and had begun to try to change dynamics in relationships, some people were becoming frustrated with her. Due to these comments, Hiedi said she decided to attempt a re-membering conversation with Kim to assist her in re-connecting to people who might be more supportive of her initiatives in her life. In doing this, Kim thought about, and later contacted, a former best friend from school days.

Hiedi had also asked whether I would review the metaphor of the migration of identity as a way to think about the process through which people try to make changes and maintain them. White (2006) has described this metaphor and particularly how he has found it useful in working with people as they have left abusive situations. Duvall and I (Duvall & Béres, 2011) have also reviewed this concept and described van Gennep's (1960) contribution to this idea through his 'rites of passage' metaphor. The metaphors of rites of passage, and migration of identity from one territory to another, provide a visual representation of the process of change. In visualizing people's journeys from one territory, or way of being, towards another territory, or another way of being, it is possible to imagine them setting sail from one land to cross an in-between, marginal or liminal space, on their way to another land. Just as migrants might leave home with mixed feelings, wanting change but sad about leaving some aspects of their homes behind, people may have mixed feelings about the changes they are initiating. They may like the thought of how things could be better when they arrive in their new country, or imagine how much better life will be once they have made changes and taken on new ways of being, but they might feel anxious during the trip and disillusioned when they arrive and circumstances are not as they had hoped. White commented that for women who were attempting to leave abusive situations, he would describe what other women had told him about how difficult this process can be and how sad they often are when they do manage to leave. This is partly why many women leave an abusive situation several times before they leave permanently, because the new way of being is not perfect either and they can experience a sense of discouragement. White said that he thought it more ethical to warn people of this process; it is not easy and straightforward. In being pre-warned of the challenges, people are less likely to blame themselves for setbacks. Nonetheless, White explained that he told women he had also heard from women who had managed to cope with the initial disappointments, and who had discovered that their situations did, in fact, improve greatly after the initial worries and discouragement. The social work or counselling process can also be thought of as a journey across the liminal space, as practitioners travel alongside people as they are making changes from one way of being to a preferred way of being. Hiedi indicated that she was pleased to review this metaphor since she had the sense that Kim wanted, at times, to turn back and give up on her journey. She thought she might share this metaphor with Kim to normalize the feelings of being betwixt and between during the process.

Following on from the discussion about the migration of identity metaphor, I asked Hiedi if she had a sense of what Kim wanted from counselling, because at this point in our conversation I was a little confused about the focus and what Kim's hopes for herself might be. I was curious to know what Hiedi had heard Kim articulate as her preferences, hopes and values in the last stage of the externalizing conversation. Hiedi said that she thought maybe Kim wanted to feel normal and went on to say, 'We want to figure out how she can manage the slips on the journey from anxiety and perfectionism to normal.' I asked Hiedi if the fact that she said 'we want' was significant. Was she assisting Kim in identifying and becoming clearer about what she wanted, or was she inadvertently taking up more of an expert role in defining goals that she thought Kim should have? She said she realized that Kim had been relieved when the 'experts' in the hospital had told her she was okay, and that Kim had begun counselling wanting Hiedi to be the expert and to tell her what to do to feel better. I asked Hiedi how she had attempted to decline this invitation to be the expert. She laughed and said that this was often a challenge for her, because she wants to help and it is exciting to work with a motivated, hard-working person who wants and completes homework and reads a great deal. I wondered how this might be part of the perfectionism that was otherwise bothering Kim and whether it might be useful to have an externalizing conversation about perfectionism. It can often be useful to have externalizing conversations about several different issues in a person's life; having had an externalizing conversation about anxiety would not necessarily mean that there were no other issues that could be externalized. This would provide a further chance to assist Kim in becoming clear about what she really wanted and preferred.

We talked about the fact that Hiedi can be an expert in the process of engaging people in narrative conversations, but as narrative practitioners it is important to find ways to decline the invitation to be experts about the content and goals of people's lives. We talked about the fact that changes made have a greater chance of being maintained if they are based on the person's hopes, dreams and preferences, rather than on goals that are generated for counselling because they seem to make sense professionally.

I also asked Hiedi if she had engaged in re-authoring conversations and wondered what the problem storyline plot and Kim's preferred storyline plot had been named. She said that her problem storyline seemed to be 'I'm not normal'. She also reiterated that Kim had indicated that her husband was normal, which is partly why she had been attracted to him. When Hiedi had asked about previous events in the 'normal' storyline, that was when Kim had described her 'different normal' experiences with friends at school. Hiedi then said that what was interesting was that Kim also now really seemed to appreciate 'different normal', making choices in her job, for instance, that put her somewhat in the margins where her work was concerned. Hiedi smiled and seemed to have a sparkle in her eyes as she described this. This made me think it might be possible that Kim also would have described this with enthusiasm and actually was more interested in moving towards a 'different normal' storyline rather than a 'normal' story-line. I asked Hiedi what she thought of this and whether this was a possibility and worth asking Kim more about. She thought it could very well be a possibility. She said, 'What I'll do ...' and then caught herself, realizing that she had slipped back into thinking about what *she* would do, rather than thinking about what Kim might want to do. She said that she would ask more about the 'normal' storyline and then again caught herself, saying, 'No, what was it? The "different normal" storyline?'

After a little more clarification about the potentially multiple storylines in Kim's life, like 'not normal' and 'normal' and possibly 'different normal',

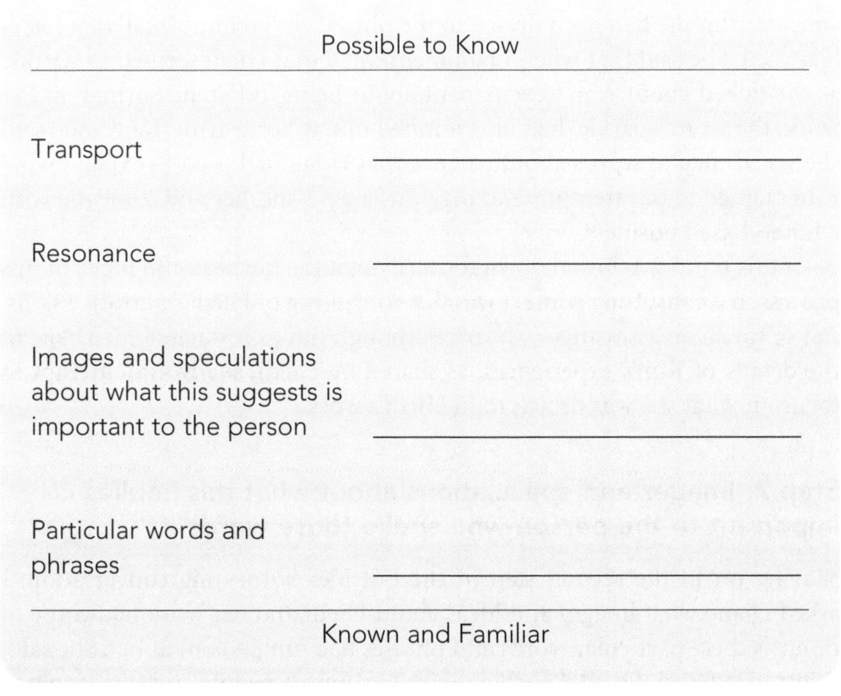

Possible to Know

Transport _____

Resonance _____

Images and speculations
about what this suggests is
important to the person _____

Particular words and
phrases _____

Known and Familiar

Figure 5.1 Outsider witnessing conversation map

Source: Adapted from White's 'Workshop Notes' posted on www.dulwichcentre.com.au

we thought we had discussed Hiedi's involvement sufficiently to move into an outsider witnessing conversation. Since Diane had offered to be the outsider witness, she had been a quiet observer of the conversation until this point. I asked if she would prefer me to interview her through the steps of the outsider witnessing conversation or to work her own way through the steps. She said that she would prefer to be interviewed.

Step 1: Particular words and phrases

The first step of this conversation involves asking the witness(es) to identify what words and phrases they were most drawn to in the conversation. A witness who is not accustomed to this type of conversation may start giving opinions and reflections very quickly, but the purpose of this stage is to assist the witness in being focused on the person who was the centre of the interview, by highlighting the actual words the person used. In asking this of Diane, she mentioned that she had been drawn to things Hiedi had said about wanting to 'do for' Kim. She said, for example, that Hiedi had said, 'I think what I'll do …', and she suggested that this seemed like a battle for Hiedi. Asking her to stick with the words and phrases Hiedi had used, rather than imagining what they implied yet, Diane said that throughout the conversation she had been drawn to the phrase 'different normal' that Hiedi had used. She said that when I had mentioned that Hiedi seemed to sparkle as she talked about Kim's excitement about being 'different normal' in her work, the word 'sparkle' had also jumped out at her. Furthermore, she said she was drawn to words about balance that Hiedi had used to explain what Kim seemed to be attempting to juggle as a wife, mother and someone with a home-based business.

   At this point we slowed down to clarify that the purpose and focus of this process in a consulting context was our consulting of Hiedi's narrative skills, not so much an assessment of Kim. Although things resonated for Diane in the details of Kim's experiences, as shared by Hiedi, she would attempt to focus on what she was drawn to in Hiedi's work.

Step 2: Images and speculations about what this implies is important to the person who spoke those words

Moving on to the second step of the outsider witnessing conversation, I asked Diane what images and ideas about Hiedi and her work had come to mind as these particular words and phrases had jumped out at her. She said, 'I just love Hiedi. She has such a desire to support people and for people to succeed to the best of their ability, and yet I have this sense this is juxtaposed with her really trying hard to just guide and not tell people what to do.' She said that was the main thing that came to mind and she couldn't think of anything else to add at that point.

Step 3: Resonance

The third step involved asking Diane what had resonated in her own life and if she had a sense of why she had been particularly drawn to the things she had mentioned in Hiedi's account of her work. This step asks the witness to link what has been heard, and responded to, to a personal account. It ensures that the witness does not slip into advice-giving from a detached position. People who have experienced witnesses responding to their conversations often suggest that part of what is so powerful about an outsider witness re-telling is the fact that the witness has been touched personally. Diane said that she had had an experience that day in her role as a child protection worker of meeting with a man who was frustrated with the Children's Aid Society's involvement and the society's focus on his alcohol use when, in fact, he thought he had had many successes in life that the society seemed to ignore totally. She said that she had been reflecting on how to manage this situation and 'give him a voice, when her agency didn't seem to want him to have a voice'. She said that she was also reflecting on the 'expert role' that she is expected to take up in her position as a child protection worker. She said that she thought that was why she had also been drawn to Hiedi's accounts of what seemed like wanting to be a helpful expert, while also not wanting to overwhelm the people with whom she works with her own ideas and enthusiasm. Although Diane's response was in regard to her work, she spoke of it in a personal manner, sharing how she was grappling, in a similar manner to Hiedi, with these challenges. This was also appropriate in this situation, because the focus of the conversation was Hiedi's professional work and so it was not unexpected that Diane would make links to her own professional work.

Step 4: Transport

The final step of the conversation offers the opportunity to reflect on how being part of the conversation has made a difference. In other words, although Diane could have been at any number of other places, she had witnessed Hiedi's descriptions of her work with Kim; what were the effects of that? I asked Diane about where this conversation had 'transported her', and whether she might think about things any differently on account of having listened to Hiedi talk about her work with Kim. Diane indicated that the conversation had reminded her of the challenges associated with being invited to be an expert and drawn into that role. She said that she would be thinking more about the need to reflect on the best ways to respond to these demands and invitations in order to centre the preferences of the 'client', or at least to acknowledge them, when in a mandated position. She also talked about feeling calmer about the fact that 'I'm not "not normal"'. She said that this felt like a gentle reminder that she wasn't put on this earth to be perfect.

The third stage of the overall conversation involves asking the first person to have been interviewed to reflect through the steps of the outsider witnessing conversation about what has just been heard. Sandy interviewed Hiedi at this point. Going through the four steps again, Sandy asked Hiedi about what words and phrases she had been drawn to; what images and ideas had come to mind about Diane because of being drawn to those phrases and images; what had resonated in her own life; and finally, where she had been transported in her thinking due to hearing and witnessing Diane's comments.

Hiedi said that the words 'different normal', 'balancing', 'juxtaposition' and 'comfort' all jumped out at her. She said that at the same time she had had an image of Kim walking through town in her black leather jacket, 'strutting her stuff' and 'looking comfortable with herself'. She said that when she heard the term 'juxtaposition' she could almost visualize the two sides of herself: the 'crazy passion' side and the 'knowledge and information' side. She also said that even as a child and young teen, she had been very interested in the idea of juxtapositions and had read science fiction books that described parallel worlds. She said that this all resonated because she went into this type of career to help people feel better and she was thinking that if Kim was comfortable with 'different normal', that would be good and she would feel a success in her journey. In terms of transport, she indicated that she was often struggling with her two sides, crazy passion and knowledge, yet she now felt more hopeful about being able to move forward. She said that she could focus on being less focused.

We then moved into a free-flowing conversation about people's observations of the whole process. Hiedi said that she had found it extremely helpful because, although she has always been aware of the juxtaposition within herself of her crazy passion and her knowledge, she found it helpful to hear this reflected back to her gently. She said that the witness re-telling of the conversation had her hearing 'similar stuff in a different way. This will help me formulate questions so as to not focus on *my* goals, but rather on hers.' As an example of this, she said she realized that at the end of the first part of the conversation she had thought of asking Kim more about when she felt 'normal', rather than 'different normal'. By the end of the re-telling process, however, she was excited to be able to ask Kim about whether 'different normal' might be of interest to her. She also said that in the past she has told people to let her know if she is overwhelming them, but that the conversation had helped her think through what else she can do so that she will not inadvertently overwhelm people.

Hiedi also sent me an email the following day to add that she had been continuing to think about the process in which we had engaged. She said, 'I really valued the outsider witnessing conversation and our style of consultation on Tuesday. I found that I got the "technical" support I needed in the beginning, but the outsider witnessing conversation provided me with more insight about my style of interacting with people I meet. I think it would be especially beneficial for experienced social workers who know the "technical" points, but feel stuck with where to go.'

Diane and Sandy also commented that they found the process useful and very different from regular supervision they receive in which they are given 'to do' lists that are checked. They said that the outsider witnessing structure provided a method of honouring their work. They agreed with Hiedi as she added a further comment about the fact that the conversation expanded ideas, rather than deflated them.

Conclusion

I do not work in a setting that has integrated post-modern thought and narrative practice throughout its structure and procedures. Within the School of Social Work, each faculty member and staff person has a different framework for understanding the world and interacting with people. Practitioners who take up narrative ways of working will also find themselves surrounded by people with different ways of looking at, and thinking about, others. Finding a method for being clear about your own preferred ways of working, while also maintaining a respectful curiosity about colleagues' ways of working, is necessary for developing and maintaining respectful relationships and the context for ongoing learning. This will contribute to the further critical reflection of practice and developments within narrative practices.

Despite wanting to be respectful of others' ways of working, I have also been committed to trying to infuse my narrative ways of working into all aspects of my work, even those that are not necessarily in direct practice with people and communities. I have, therefore, provided an overview in this chapter of ways in which it might be possible to integrate narrative ideas into agency-based work, note taking, report writing and team consultations. Conducting workshops and presentations will sometimes also be required of practitioners in agency-based work, and these can be influenced by narrative practices as well. In discussing the role of critical reflection of practice as a form of inquiry in the next chapter, which at times results in presenting findings, I will discuss some considerations regarding conducting presentations.

Finally, I wish to reiterate that I am grateful for Walter Bera's generosity in sharing the forms and approaches that the Kenwood Center uses. I hope that these might be useful for other people who are thinking about how to integrate narrative ideas more fully into their agency procedures. He has indicated that if people wish to consult him for assistance in adjusting the forms for their practice contexts, or to request updated forms, they may contact him at the Kenwood Center.

Notes

1. This is a nice example of a form of copying that originates, as discussed in the Preface and Chapter 1.

2. http://www.kenwoodcenter.org provides a description of the Kenwood Center with links to details of workshops and narrative books.

3. I have included the Narrative Individual Family Questionnaire (NIFQ) 1 and 2 that Walter shared with me in Appendices 1 and 2 respectively.

4. I have included this form in Appendix 3.

5. I have included this form in Appendix 4.

6. I have included the description and diagram of the narragram in Appendix 5. Bera's narragram is yet another example of copying that originates, influenced by the conversation maps and also opening up new creative practices within narrative therapy.

6 Critical Reflection as Inquiry and Practice-Based Evidence

Introduction

I became interested in both critical theory and narrative practice at the same time. This came about partly as a result of beginning my doctoral research in a critical pedagogy and cultural studies specialization, after my research interest had developed from reflecting on practice. It was while I was pursuing my doctoral work that I first read Schön (1983) and Fook (1999, 2000) and recognized the value of their approaches to reflecting on practice for the further development of practice theory and knowledge. As I was reading Giroux and Simon (1989), hooks (1994) and Freire (1970) in the area of critical pedagogy, I began to recognize the influences of critical social theory across the fields of education and social work. At the same time, I was becoming fascinated by the post-modern and post-structural elements of narrative practice and later realized the commonalities within both narrative practice and Fook's approach to critical reflection of practice, partly because of these elements. Fook, in an interview presented in Béres, Bowles and Fook (2011), clarifies why it is that critical reflection looks so similar to narrative practice, saying that it is because both draw on the same broader theories and approaches:

> The ideas of Foucault, for instance, have been used by many different disciplines and in different ways and have gotten filtered into those disciplines in a way that they think they are separate kinds of things, but in fact a lot of the socially based disciplines use particular theories anyway. So all I've done with critical reflection is taken it and theorized it a bit further, using post-modern and post-structural ideas and grafted them on to Brookfield. So my version of critical reflection just happens to use some Foucault, which makes it look like narrative therapy, but I also use Brookfield which makes it look like education. (Béres, Bowles & Fook, 2011, pp. 85–6)

Brookfield (1995), who has influenced Fook in the development of critical reflection of practice, begins the first chapter of his book *Becoming a*

Critically Reflective Teacher by saying that 'we teach to change the world' (p. 1). Many social workers would probably suggest that they practise social work to also try to change the world and make a positive difference. Brookfield goes on to say that despite our attempts to increase the amount of love and social justice in the world, we cannot be sure that even sincere intentions are smoothly transferred into appropriate practice appreciated by everyone; good intentions do not guarantee good or effective practices. He suggests that it is naïve to think this and therefore that it is necessary to reflect critically on our practice in order to identify underlying assumptions and check with others about how we are coming across to them. As Epston (2008) reminds us, 'Michael [White] lived by a quote of Foucault's: we know what we do, we think we know what we think, but do we know what what we do does?' (p. 4). He goes on to say that White was primarily interested in what those people and communities who consulted him judged of his work, rather than in professional colleagues' judgements.

It is important to take responsibility for our actions and practices and to make sure that we are having the effect we want to have on others. At the same time, agencies and organizations are required to respond to demands for accountability in the use of funding. Partly as a result of the need to show effectiveness and the appropriate use of resources, practitioners have needed to demonstrate that they are using evidence-based practices and to prove that goals of practice are being reached in a timely fashion.

What has been particularly challenging about these demands is the resulting over-reliance on a particular form of evidence that is constructed by mainstream discourses about what constitutes reliable proof; these discourses also privilege expert-driven, technical-rational approaches to research. Not only is it difficult for practitioners to engage in the large-scale research projects that would be considered the gold standard, with large numbers of randomly selected participants and control groups, these discourses are firmly rooted in modernist claims that are not consistent with the philosophical and political underpinnings of narrative practices and critical social theory. This has meant that for narrative practitioners who have made the paradigm shift from mainstream modernist influences, and who are committed to post-modern and post-structural practice and ethics, there has been the added concern of how to address the need for proof, accountability and research in a manner that is congruent with their professional and philosophical posture.

Payne and Askeland (2008), describing the contributions of 'postcolonialism and postmodernism' (p. 9) to considerations of globalization, have suggested that there are a range of different types of post-modern thinkers and practitioners. Just as Harrison and Melville (2010) refer to Midgley as 'adopting an air of pessimism' (p. 31) when suggesting that few social workers are seeking to understand international social work, I have come to think of post-modern authors on a continuum of pessimism to optimism. While all post-modernist thinkers will engage in critiquing modernist thinking and practice, the pessimistic thinkers do not appear to have an alternative practice to offer. The more optimistic post-modernists are better able also to offer possibilities; they reflect on their practice and want to improve it. I am concerned by the rigidity that can come about from an over-reliance on technical-rational knowledge, but I am also concerned about the need to engage ethically with people and ensure that our practices are effective; I think I might be described as optimistic as well as post-modern. As Payne and Askeland also point out, reflexivity is crucial, 'placing ourselves and our interpretation in the action' (2008, p. 28). Critical reflection of practice is an approach to reflection that is congruent with narrative practice, incorporates reflexivity and has the potential to be a form of inquiry that holds us accountable and generates new practice wisdom.

The Munro Review (Munro, 2011) points out:

Analytic skills can be enhanced by formal teaching and reading. Intuitive skills are essentially derived from experience. Experience on its own, however, is not enough. It needs to be allied to reflection – time and attention given to mulling over the experience and learning from it. This is often best achieved in conversation with others, in supervision for example, or in discussions with colleagues. Michael Oakeshott draws attention to the limitations of a 'crowded' life where people are continually occupied and engaged but have no time to stand back and think. A working life given over to distracted involvement does not allow for the integration of experience. (p. 90)

Acknowledging the various criticisms of the term 'evidence-based practice', the Munro Review suggests using the term in a broad sense to mean 'drawing on the best available evidence to inform practice at all stages of the work *and* of integrating that evidence with the social worker's own understanding of the child and family's circumstances and their *values and preferences*' (p. 95, italics mine), rather than merely adding certain researched approaches into a professional bag of tricks. I have stressed here the use of the child and family's values and preferences alongside the professional's understanding, since this is consistent with narrative practices that strive to privilege these aspects of people's lives. This description also clearly stresses how important it is that the evidence practitioners draw on is relevant for all stages of work with people rather than only informing certain aspects. It is not useful in the long term to be able to conduct and write speedy and sophisticated risk assessments with theoretically grounded descriptions of the development of problems and yet not to know what to do next in practice. The Munro Review points out that 'this omission is grave' (p. 136). Critical reflection of practice may provide a method for filling this gap.

Positioning narrative therapy as a practice of critical social theory

Fook (2003) describes the influence of earlier forms of radical social work in the United Kingdom and more recent contributions from Canada and Australia to the development of what is now considered critical social work. What the various forms of radical and critical social work have in common, she suggests, is a structural analysis of personal problems, combined with a critique of the potentially social control aspects of social work, and a commitment to personal liberation alongside social change. Underlying these approaches and commitments are key aspects of critical social theory, which she reviews, including the following principle:

> The need to develop ways of knowing which transcend the dominant constructed ways of knowing, including the recognition that knowledge may reflect 'empirical reality' but is also socially constructed. Self-reflection and interaction therefore become important processes in creating knowledge, and this places emphasis on the transformative potential of communication processes themselves. (Fook, 2003, pp. 124–5)

This principle of critical social theory is congruent with narrative practice commitments, which also recognize the social construction of reality and the need for transformation. What has been a challenge for narrative practitioners, and Fook would suggest for radical and critical social workers influenced by critical social theory, is finding a way of reflecting on and researching practice that acknowledges and takes these concerns into consideration.

White, when he consulted with me on the development of a research project in 2007, indicated that he had previously been hesitant to research his practices in mainstream ways, and had been frustrated by the technical-rational approach to attempting to prove effectiveness objectively. He seemed to imply a suspicion of academic researchers, setting themselves up as objective experts, accessing research funding, conducting pre and post measurements or setting up control groups, and then writing articles that would benefit their own academic careers more than the people who were receiving the services that were being studied. However, at the same time, he also acknowledged that as he trained people in narrative practices, they were beginning more often to tell him that, although they preferred working from a narrative perspective because of the ethics and the positive effects in people's lives that they observed, they were being urged by their managers and employers to use other approaches that had been researched more and were described as 'evidence-based' forms of practice. He was, due to these concerns, supportive of, and interested in, assisting with developing an approach to researching narrative practices that was congruent with the principles of narrative practice. This was why he was excited by the idea of not only measuring pre and post scores for people engaged in services, but also asking both the 'service users' and 'service providers' to comment on the experience of the process of therapy and the effects of being involved in this type of practice. By including the voices and comments of everyone involved in the practice, a more complete description can be generated, and the concerns related to the effects of the process also addressed.[1] This style of research responds to the concerns raised by critical social theorists and prac-titioners, providing one way of potentially filling some of the theory–practice gap with which people in the field continue to grapple. Social and health services research must generate knowledge that is useful for ongoing practice. Although there is a long and important tradition of generating theories and testing hypotheses, it is important also to privilege the types of knowledge and practice skills that can be generated from critically reflective practice.

Fook (2000) says that, despite the fact that social work has prided itself on being a profession that focuses on the integration of theory and practice, further distances have continued developing between the two areas. She points out that post-modern analysis has created a context in which 'it is more acceptable to question the taken-for-granted authority of academic researchers' (p. 107). Raising questions, therefore, about what is legitimate as social work knowledge and who should generate it, she moves on to report on findings from studies that she conducted with Martin Ryan and Linette Hawkins. The main study she discusses was one conducted with 30 experi-enced social workers. They compared the findings from this study with find-ings from a study conducted with beginning practitioners. Whereas recent graduates were more likely to attempt to apply theories they had learnt in textbooks and to do so deductively, the experienced practitioners demon-strated the ability to develop theory inductively. Fook indicates that experi-enced practitioners 'do not appear to fit the more "scientific" orientation indicated by modernist notions of expertise' (p. 114). She goes on to say that they do not begin engagement with people with a preconceived notion that the goals of service should be based on professional knowledge and theory, but rather with a commitment to a mutual process that entails self-discov-ery for both the practitioner and the person receiving services, which is clearly consistent with narrative practices. She concludes by saying:

In a time of postmodern crisis we need to frame professional expertise as grounded and contextual, involving transferable (rather than generalisable) knowledge and the ability to create this through reflective and reflexive processes. In this way expert professional social workers are able to create critical knowledge which potentially challenges and resists current forms of domination, and they are able to maintain commitment to a system of social values which allow them to work with, yet transcend the contradictions and uncertainties of daily practice. (2000, p. 118)

Critical reflection of practice as a form of inquiry and practice-based evidence

Fook and Gardner (2007) provide a clear and practical handbook for developing the skills of practising critical reflection. They provide descriptions of the underlying theories that have contributed to the development of critical reflection of practice, define the terms and then lay out the steps involved in learning about practice assumptions and generating new practice theory by deconstructing incidents within practice. Critical reflection of practice is influenced by Schön's model of reflecting *in* and reflecting *on* practice; an understanding of the need for reflexivity, which is described as recognizing the effect of the self of the researcher on the research; and post-modernism and post-structuralism. All this combines with critical social theory to include an awareness of personal and structural power and the influence of discourses of power and knowledge.

The process of critical reflection of practice involves, usually in a group setting, discussion, de-construction and re-construction of a critical incident. What Fook and Gardner mean by a critical incident is merely a story of practice that has stayed with the person, rather than an incident that necessarily involved a crisis or problem. In North America at least, 'critical incident' has begun to be associated with 'critical incident debriefing' and needing to provide support and counselling to people who have been negatively affected due to a crisis: a shooting or a suicide in a school, or the death of a child in care, for example. In contrast, for the purposes of critical reflection of practice, practitioners are asked to think of an incident they could describe that has remained with them as a significant event in their recent memories for some reason. It could be that the memory is of a practice event when something went particularly well and the person is especially proud of the moment, but unsure why it turned out so well. Alternatively, it could be a memory of a practice event that continues to bother the person because it did not go well, resulting in ongoing discomfort regarding the outcome and confusion about what could have been done differently. It could just as easily be regarding a situation with colleagues, or something outside of the work situation altogether, that has remained prominent in the person's mind.

It is important that practitioners who describe a critical incident describe the story; the context; what was done within that context; and also the effects of this on themselves, rather than describing a case study, which is what many practitioners are more accustomed to presenting. Practitioners are asked to focus primarily on the effects of the incident on themselves in order to understand why the incident has remained prominent in their thinking. For example, if the incident involved telling a story of meeting with colleagues in order to address a concern, and the satisfaction involved in the process and results of the meeting, the primary focus would be on the effects of this on the person telling the story, even though there would also have been effects on the other people who are described as being part of the story.

Through critically reflecting on the incident, practitioners move into an examination and deconstruction of the underlying assumptions and taken-for-granteds within the story that is being recounted. This can be accomplished much more readily when this process occurs in a group setting, or at least with one other person, since it is often difficult to see what our own taken-for-granted assumptions are, since we have become so accustomed to them. In terms of the example where someone is happy about how a meeting resulted in understanding and a satisfactory response to a concern, perhaps an assumption regarding the importance and value of clear communication is being raised and reinforced. Rather than complaining to colleagues who have no ability to address the concerns, perhaps the incident points out the value of clear decision-making about whom it would be most important to involve in discussions, and the necessity for respectful and clear descriptions of the situation.

The process of critical reflection of practice does not end with deconstructing the incident and discovering hidden assumptions, but rather continues to the point where reconstructing also occurs in the form of more explicit descriptions of potentially successful practice, so that theory develops from practice and then has the opportunity to inform further practice.[2] This is consistent with the idea of optimistic post-modernism, since it does contribute to a recommitment to ongoing best practice and potentially the development of new ways of working.

What is particularly useful, in responding to the concerns I have raised about what would be an appropriate research approach for narrative practices, is that Fook and Gardner (2007) also describe the process of using critical reflection in research and evaluation. They clarify that although research can be defined 'as a process of systematic investigation leading to increased understanding of a phenomenon or issue of interest' (Stringer and Dwyer in

Fook and Gardner, 2007, p. 162), evaluation more usually regards investigating the effectiveness of an intervention. Fook and Gardner describe the debates regarding evidence-based practice and the various approaches to suggesting what it constitutes. What they argue for, and provide a method for, is building research and evaluation into ongoing practice. Critical reflection offers a framework for practitioners to stand back from their practice in order to pay attention to it in a systematic way, look at it from different angles and develop new practice theory and skills.

For practitioners who are worried about having to develop their research skills, or finding time to conduct large-scale research projects, critical reflection offers a method of inquiry that is easily integrated into ongoing practice and contributes to the growing interest in practice-based research.

Critical best practice and practice-based evidence

Ferguson (2003) has outlined a critical best practice perspective for research that develops a methodology that moves away from a deficit perspective, also drawing on critical theory to promote learning from practice, generating what he calls 'practice-based evidence' (p. 1005). Using a case study from a large-scale study conducted in the United Kingdom, he demonstrates how this critical best practice approach and analysis can assist practitioners in developing a further understanding of how they work creatively within certain structures to bring about positive effects and changes in people's lives. He suggests that what he calls critical best practice combines four aspects:

1. Identifying the best practice that is occurring. [*This is similar to choosing a positive critical incident in Fook and Gardner's (2007) approach to critical reflection of practice.*]
2. The use of critical theory for analysis of what is occurring. [*This is also consistent with Fook and Gardner's approach.*]
3. A commitment to producing scientifically sound data about what works well. [*This allows it to contribute to 'evidence-based practice'.*]
4. The inclusion of knowledge from practice experience, which is like 'practice-based evidence' and includes descriptions of the process and social action. [*This is consistent with suggestions I have presented earlier about the need to focus on more than merely the outcome measurements in evaluation.*]

As Ferguson suggests, it is crucial that practitioners develop these forms of critically reflective practice and methods for producing descriptions and evidence of best practice. In the United Kingdom in particular, he points out, the Department of Health in 1998 and the Social Care Institute of Excellence in 2001 have asserted the need for professions like social work to be 'based less on "opinions" and much more on data about "what works"' (Ferguson, 2003, p. 1006). He goes on to suggest that this must include contributions from the range of people involved in social care and professional practice, meaning that 'service users' need to be involved as well in contributing their opinions. This is clearly also consistent with the commitments of narrative practice, post-modern and strength-based approaches to practice.

The one case that Ferguson (2003) presents from the larger research project in order to provide an example of a critical best practice approach involves a public health nurse who made a referral to a social worker due to concerns about the neglect and lack of supervision of two small children by a single mother who relied on an under-age babysitter when she worked night shifts. Despite the mother's initial defensiveness and the demands by the Child Protection Committee to monitor the situation and stay involved, the social worker and mother developed an effective and trusting working relationship and the case was closed seven months later. Rather than merely focusing on the outcome – the case was successful – Ferguson points out that the critical best practice perspective, like critical reflection of practice, provides a manner for learning about the practice and process that contributed to the positive outcome. In reflecting on this particular situation, Ferguson describes the social worker's creative and critically reflective stance as integrating feminist, Marxist and 'social policy analysis, in terms of a critique of motherhood, inequality and the demands of parenting in poverty, but in a manner which is grounded in a use of counselling methods to establish trust and begin a supportive, therapeutic relationship' (p. 1015). Ferguson provides further discussion and details of this particular case, suggesting that what is most clear is the potential for creative anti-oppressive practice within structures that can otherwise appear overly bureaucratic, and that in reflecting on this type of practice it is possible to support and further develop these important practice skills and theory.

The potential benefits of multi-methodology

Fook (2002), although suggesting critical reflection of incidents within practice, has also discussed the benefits of an inclusive approach to social work research. In considering the possibilities of generating theory from practice, she suggests that there are many approaches that can be used to access practice experience. It is humbling to remind ourselves that there are numerous research methodologies across the disciplines and that as post-modern practitioners we do not need to create, or re-create, forms of inquiry, but rather learn from and incorporate many and various approaches. Ethnographic and observational methods, review of documents and accounts of practice (interviews or recordings) are all possible. Participatory action research and action research are particularly appropriate for addressing the need to inform practice and involve all participants in reflecting on practice. Fook then goes on to describe different ways of analysing the data where the collected data is made up of descriptions of the practice experiences that have been gathered in one of the methods suggested. This can be done deductively, which involves applying previously developed theory to describe and understand the data, or inductively, which involves the development of theory from the data. Both quantitative and qualitative approaches can be used for the analysis, separately or in a mixed-methods approach. I would add, also, that it is important when working with Indigenous and marginalized groups to consult with people in those groups about what would constitute the most appropriate and ethical forms of inquiry (Lassiter, 2005; Tuhiwai Smith, 1999; Wilson, 2008).

Whether to use quantitative or qualitative methodology, deductive or inductive, observational or interview approaches is dependent on the purpose of the research and whether there are specific questions to answer and what types of questions they are. 'How' questions are more likely to require more descriptive and qualitative forms of research, whereas 'which' questions could be more quantitative in nature: for instance, 'How do people make meaning of, and respond to, a narrative therapy interview?' versus 'Which type of drug or treatment approach is more effective?' One approach is not better than another, but rather better for answering particular questions.

In proposing critical reflection of practice, combined with ideas from the critical best practice perspective, I am suggesting that practitioners can reflect on their practice, include input from people who have been engaged in the practice, and contribute to practice-based evidence that can inform ongoing practice. I am not suggesting that other forms of research and inquiry are inappropriate.

None of us can have all the skills, or the interest, necessary to conduct all forms of research. Fook (2002), for instance, suggests that some people are better with numbers and fine details, whereas others seem natural at connecting ideas and themes. Since life and professional practice are complex, she goes on to say that we require many perspectives and different research capabilities in order to understand the complexity. It may be that teams of researchers with various skills are best suited for some larger-scale studies, and that collaborative co-researchers can provide a richer and more detailed description of practice contexts, processes and outcomes. No one person, whether practitioner, 'service-user' or researcher, has the purest point of view, and so being humble and transparent about our own position, and including other perspectives, is going to be helpful in generating knowledge that is more likely to be transferable.

Disseminating knowledge

Ethical research must result in dissemination of the new knowledge developed through the project. A web-based ethics guidebook developed by the Institute of Education, University of London, UK, defines dissemination as literally meaning '*sowing seeds*' and points out that it 'goes beyond publication of your research. Research may aim to sow the seeds of change in policies, services, or belief about whatever has been studied.'[3] The guide goes on to indicate that 'people have an ethical duty to try and make their research findings widely known, and, if possible, acted upon'. Furthermore, it also presents a discussion regarding the need to consider the impact of research, as well as its dissemination. Suggestions are presented that indicate a growing acceptance of the range of possible types of dissemination in order to increase the level of impact, and the guide continues, 'As the importance of dissemination and impact becomes increasingly recognised, researchers are using ever more innovative methods – including websites, video conference, drama, and even exhibitions.'

In the Tri-Council's policy statements, which guide ethical research practices in Canada, dissemination is also highlighted as a crucial aspect of research, especially when it has involved people as research participants in the project. These policy statements are consistent with the UK statements, indicating:

> To justify the involvement of participants, and the risks and other burdens they are asked to bear, research must be valuable. That is, it must have a reasonable likelihood of promoting social good. If research findings and the research material and data they are based upon, are not disseminated … within a reasonable time, their value may be diminished or lost, betraying the contributions and sacrifices of participants. (http://www.pre.ethics.gc.ca/eng/policy-politique/initiatives/tcps2-eptc2/chapter11-chapitre11/#toc11-1e)

Bruce Thyer, a Fulbright Scholar, recently spent two weeks visiting the School of Social Work in which I teach in Canada. He is a professor at the Florida State University College of Social Work and editor of the journal *Research on Social Work Practice*. He spent most of his time during the two weeks with us meeting with individual faculty members and providing research and publication consultation to the social work community. I admitted to him at his farewell lunch that I had been a little worried about his visit, since he is a great supporter of evidence-based research and behaviour therapy. I worried that we would not have much in common, but in fact we shared a commitment to ethical and effective practice. I appreciated the manner in which he described types of inquiry and the range of approaches to disseminating results. I found his thoughts helpful for practitioners as well as people engaged in research and academic careers. He suggested that single-case research designs and descriptions of practice could be valuable and worth publishing. He also encouraged practitioners and researchers alike to 'just write'. He said that for people beginning their careers, it might not be expected that they would have articles published right away in highly regarded peer-reviewed research journals, but that they could begin by writing letters to editors of newspapers and professional magazines or book reviews. Websites and YouTube videos were also suggested during his presentation as possible venues for sharing the results of research projects.

I am currently involved in the beginning stages, having only just received approval from the necessary research ethics review boards, for a participatory action research project with a group of Indigenous and non-Indigenous children and parents. Due to the history of appropriation of Indigenous knowledge in North America, as well as in other parts of the world, it was crucial for my Indigenous colleagues that the raw data not be disseminated widely, since there was the potential for it to be misused. However, a participatory action research design is particularly structured in order for the data collected to be reviewed by the research team to inform the ongoing development of the programme being studied: in this case a pen-pal project in the school system. Although the data may not be disseminated widely, it will have an impact on the further development of the programme. It also has the potential for highlighting aspects of the work that could bring about further research that could be disseminated more widely.

Although there is a greater acceptance of a variety of methods of dissemination of findings, it continues to be possible that practitioners involved in critical reflection of practice, whether of best practice or of critical incidents, will be required to present their work to their colleagues or in conference or workshop settings.

There are numerous opportunities for training in presentation skills. Most of this training will review the use of PowerPoint slides: for instance, do not include too much text on each slide; use images as well as text; be clear about the objectives of the presentation; summarize and review what has been presented. I attended a workshop regarding teaching in higher education settings when I first took up my academic position and remember the women being told to wear suits and look professional in order to be

respected by students. This has not seemed like particularly useful or necessary advice, but could be due to my working in a social work programme;
perhaps it would be appropriate in other disciplines. However, what is not
usually reviewed in this type of training is any reflection regarding the
modelling of practice skills, or philosophical stance, through the style of
presentation.

When I first took up my position as a faculty member and began teaching
in a university setting following early training in narrative practices, I found
it challenging to maintain the de-centred position that had become part of
my narrative practitioner posture. I have written about my reflections on
these early teaching experiences, including reflections from students, in the
journal *Radical Pedagogy* (Béres et al., 2008). I came to the conclusion that
when students, and people attending conferences or training workshops, pay
to learn new material and skills, they are not going to be very impressed with
presenters who abdicate their expertise and knowledge by taking up a 'not-
knowing' stance in order to centre the others' knowledge. As I have been
moving to a greater awareness of the stance within narrative practice that
allows for an expertise in practice while also moving away from suggesting an
expertise in knowing about others' lives, I have also been able to take up a
similar position in teaching and presenting. I feel more comfortable now
acknowledging my skills and training as I also point out that the students, or
audience members, have knowledge and skills. I have modelled this in one of
the entry-level undergraduate classes I teach by engaging students in mindfulness exercises as a method of beginning to reflect on their own knowledge,
thoughts and reactions. This is consistent with a narrative perspective that
uses the skills of narrative practice to assist people in becoming more
comfortable with their values and preferences and clearer about what aspects
of their work are already in line with those preferences. If they want to learn
and develop new skills, they can incorporate them into practices that are
already consistent with their preferred ways of working. Although I have seen
people struggle at times with what can seem to be a paradigm shift as they
move from one philosophy of practice to another, they usually already have
a set of skills in relationship building, empathy and listening that can be
further supported and used within a new paradigm. It is important, therefore, to honour what people know and what is working, even as we present
new ideas. This involves integrating ideas from adult education (Brookfield,
1995) and critical pedagogy (Giroux and Simon, 1989; hooks, 1994).

Conclusion

What I have attempted to argue for in this chapter is that assuming our
practice is having the effects we wish for is not enough: we need to find ways

to examine the effects, asking others also to examine the effects, since good intentions are not sufficient (Chambon, 1999, p. 65). If we want to engage in ethical and effective practice, we need to integrate ethical and effective of reflection and inquiry into our practice, and also include the voices ple who are engaged in these practices with us.

he Munro Review (Munro, 2011) suggests the need for reflection of practice in order to develop professional confidence and expertise. Payne (2006) proposes asking people regularly whether the services they are receiving are acceptable, as a form of de-centring ourselves. Ruch, Turney and Ward (2010) indicate the need for reflective practice and supervision to ensure appropriate relationships in social work and counselling situations. Finding methods for integrating reflection into practice, however, has sometimes been a challenge for busy practitioners.

I recently had the opportunity for further discussion with Walter Bera regarding the questionnaires used at the Kenwood Center, which I described in the previous chapter and which are included in Appendices 1 to 5. He commented that by using these forms, people receiving services are able to comment on what is working for them in the counselling process and what they would like changed. His comments highlighted that the consistent use of these types of questionnaires is not only a method for including the voices of people in the actual practice process, but also for engaging people in the ongoing reflection of practice as a form of inquiry that can influence and shape future practices with future people. The results of questionnaires can be reviewed with those who completed the questionnaires, as well as reviewed in team consultation, supervision and for programme evaluation and research projects.

In this chapter I have reviewed critical social theory and post-modern critiques of traditional technical-rational forms of research and knowledge creation, and presented forms of inquiry more consistent with the post-modern practice of narrative therapy. I hope that practitioners will be inspired by the possibilities offered by Fook and Gardner's (2007) form of critical reflection of practice and Ferguson's (2003) thoughts regarding a critical best practice perspective for research. Integrating all that these approaches offer assists with developing a better understanding of, and building on, what is already working well in practice.

These approaches to critically reflecting on our practice will proceed to inform our, and hopefully others', practice. Finally within this chapter, I have also presented thoughts regarding the need to disseminate knowledge in order to share ideas with others, since, as Fook (2000) has suggested, these forms of knowledge can be transferable, if not generalizable. Many various and creative ways for 'publishing' findings are developing; critically reflective narrative practitioners will only be limited by their own imaginations.

Notes

1. This was a research project on which Duvall was a co-researcher and on which White, and later Epston, consulted. The purpose of this research was to involve both 'service providers' and 'service users' on reflecting on pivotal moments within the process of the service in addition to examining pre, post and follow-up questionnaires. This was in order to examine the effects on everyone involved of being part of a narrative conversation. We were aware that if an examination of the process was not included, it could be possible to show effectiveness based on change in scores on a particular measurement, but people could still be affected by the process (positively or negatively) in addition to those specific scores. We drew on Toukmanian and Rennie (1992) in considering how to research the process of therapy.

2. See Fook and Gardner (2007) for a full description of this process since I do not have the space in one chapter to do it appropriate justice. For instance, they discuss the need for safety in group discussions and what types of questions assist with unpacking assumptions versus merely engaging in problem-solving discussions.

3. http://www.ethicsguidebook.ac.uk/Dissemination-and-impact-144. This website was funded by the Economic and Social Research Council through the Researcher Development Initiative.

7 Spirituality and Narrative Practice: Listening for the 'Little Sacraments of Daily Existence'

Introduction

I recently had the opportunity to meet with social workers, nurse practitioners, doctors and counsellors in the United Kingdom at the British Association for Studies in Spirituality conference (2012). Many of the practitioners, academics and researchers were raising questions about how to address issues of spirituality competently in direct practice with people. Only a month later I attended a similar gathering of delegates at a joint Canadian and American Associations of Social Work and Spirituality conference (2012). The social workers at the second conference were reflecting on the manner in which their interests in spirituality seemed to position them somewhat in the margins of mainstream social work, despite the growing interest in spirituality in social work over the past 10 years. They also were considering how best to integrate spirituality into practice, with a range of approaches being considered. As Holloway (2007) points out, 'the evidence base is growing for the significance for large numbers of people of a dimension which they term "spiritual", and a set of issues whose existential source remains untouched by standard psycho-social therapeutic techniques' (p. 275). She points out that despite the fact that the majority of social work professionals may be less religious and spiritual than the general public, it behoves us to be able to work sensitively with people who have religious and spiritual beliefs. This is an element of culturally sensitive practice.

While attending these conferences, I reflected on how well narrative therapy is able to address spirituality in practice, offering a respectful, non-judgemental and non-directive approach to working with issues related to spirituality and meaning-making. This provides a method for practitioners who would otherwise be uncomfortable with raising issues related to religion or spirituality to begin to open up spaces for people to speak about what gives them a sense of meaning and purpose.

I will begin this chapter by presenting broad definitions of spirituality. I will then describe Celtic spirituality, which shares much in common with growing interests in eco-spirituality and concerns with 'place', providing examples from research interviews. I will touch on the concept of hospitality as it connects to both spirituality and direct practice, and conclude the chapter with a case example.

Defining spirituality

There are a few definitions of spirituality that I have found useful and that can provide a starting point for considering how to integrate spirituality into practice. Canda's (1988) definition of spirituality has been particularly influential internationally. He defines it as 'the human quest for personal meaning and mutually fulfilling relationships among people, the non human environment, and, for some, God' (p. 243). Crisp (2010) provides the following definition:

> Spirituality involves an awareness of the other, which may be God or other human or divine beings, or something else, which provides the basis for us to establish our needs and desires for, understand our experiences of, and ask questions about, meaning, identity, connectedness, transformation and transcendence. While for some individuals these concerns will be integrally associated with their religious beliefs, and may only make sense within a specific religious framework, meaning, identity, connectedness, transformation and transcendence are intrinsic to the human experience, whether or not individuals regard these to be in the realm of spirituality. Most, if not all, of these concerns are, or arguably should be, issues of relevance to social work. (Crisp, 2010, p. 7)

Both of these definitions highlight that spirituality is about what gives a sense of purpose and meaning to a person's life. For some this might include a relationship with the Divine, but that is not true for everyone. For some it might include involvement in a formal religion and religious community for worship and fellowship and perhaps a commitment to social justice, but this is also not true for everyone. It is interesting that Crisp argues that these issues are intrinsic to people's experiences and that Canda stresses the importance of the non-human environment for some people's experiences of spirituality, since these are two issues that I wish to highlight.

Since narrative therapy focuses on privileging how people who consult us make meaning of the stories of their lives, and also assists people in making their own judgements about what they would prefer for their lives based on their sense of meaning and purpose, hope and preferences, narrative practices seem particularly well suited to dealing with issues of spirituality if spirituality is defined the way Canda (1988) and Crisp (2010) have defined it. Practitioners I met in England were particularly concerned by the fact that in situations where particular types of checklists are relied on to assist with assessments, practitioners might too easily rely on merely asking about whether or not a person has a religious affiliation, believing that they have therefore asked about the person's spirituality. If spirituality, however, is about meaning and purpose, questions will need to be asked that assist people in reflecting on what gives them a sense of meaning, rather than only asking about religious affiliation. Holloway and Moss (2010) represent the relationship between meaning and purpose, spirituality and religion by presenting a simple diagram of three concentric circles. The smallest circle is drawn with a dotted line, in which 'R' is placed to represent 'Religion'. This is situated within a larger circle in which 'S' is placed for 'Spirituality'. These two circles are put within a larger circle labelled 'Meaning and purpose'. They label this diagram 'Spirituality as an inclusive concept' (Holloway & Moss, 2010, p. 30). They suggest that spirituality is a form of meaning and purpose for many people, and that religion is a form of both spirituality and meaning and purpose for a smaller group of people, where there is a porous relationship between experiences of religion and experiences of spirituality.

Cook, Powell and Sims of the Royal College of Psychiatrists (2009) in the United Kingdom suggest that there is a need in practice settings to add to the usual bio-psychosocial mode of thought a fourth dimension: that of spirituality. They use Cook's definition of spirituality:

> Spirituality is a distinctive, potentially creative and universal dimension of human experience arising from both within the inner subjective awareness of individuals and within communities, social groups and traditions. It may be experienced as relationship with that which is intimately 'inner', immanent and personal, within the self and others, and/or as relationship with that which is wholly 'other', transcendent and beyond the self. It is experienced as being fundamental or ultimate importance and is thus concerned with matters of meaning and purpose in life, truth and values. (Cook, Powell & Sims, 2009, p. 4)

Cook's definition of spirituality is consistent with those provided by both Canda and Crisp, also suggesting that spirituality is intrinsic, or universal; in addition, he distinguishes between immanent and ascendant forms of spirituality, which is something that Michael White identifies in an interview published in 2000. White points out that he believes there are at least three different ways of thinking about spirituality:

1. Ascendant, which involves looking 'up' and 'out' there to the Divine as a way to guide our lives.

2. Immanent, involving looking inside or 'down deep', which could be considered as more psychological in manner. This can involve believing that there is some sort of 'true' human nature and that the more closely we become our 'true' selves the more spiritual we will also become.
3. Immanent/ascendant, which involves a connection to one's soul or the Divine spark deep within oneself as a way to become more in touch with a God that is ascendant.

White, however, goes on to note that what interests him more than these three versions of spirituality is what he chooses to call the spirituality of the surface, having to do with material existence. This could also be considered a spirituality that is linked to the physical environment. He says:

> When I talk about spirituality I am not appealing to the divine or the holy. And I am not saluting human nature, whatever that might be, if it exists at all. The notion of spirituality that I am relating to is one that makes it possible for me to see and to appreciate the visible in people's lives, not the invisible … it is a spirituality that has to do with relating to one's material options in a way that one becomes more conscious of one's own knowing. (White, 2000, p. 132)

He goes on to suggest that this form of spirituality is one that concerns itself with personal ethics, modes of being and thought, and is most related to the 'sort of spirituality to which Foucault referred in his work on the ethics of the self' (p. 133).

Later on in the same interview, White is asked again about what it is he is attempting to listen to when he listens in therapeutic conversations, because Hoyt, one of the interviewers, had commented earlier that this seemed particularly unique and special in White's work that he had witnessed. He said that White seemed to have the skill of being able to see something holy or special in people, even when they had done miserable things, or hurt and abused others. Hoyt commented that this reminded him of how in India people put their hands together and say 'Namaste – "I salute the divine in you" – meaning "Whatever the story on the surface is, I see something holy or special"' (White, 2000, p. 130). Chittister (2004[1994]) also mentions 'Namaste' when she quotes Ram Das as indicating '"Namaste" … means: I honor the place within you where the entire universe resides; I honor the place in you of love, of light, of truth, of peace. I honor the place within you where if you are in that place in you and I am in that place in me, there is only one of us' (p. 141). In returning to this comment and question, White quotes from the poet David Malouf's work, *The Great World*:

[T]he little sacraments of daily existence, movements of the heart and invitations of the close but inexpressible grandeur and terror of things, … [are] the major part of what happens every day in the life of the planet, and [have] been from the very beginning. To find words for *that*; to make glow with significance what is usually unseen, and unspoken to: that, when it occurs, is what binds us all, since it speaks immediately out of the centre of each one of us; giving shape to what we too have experienced and did not till then have words for, though as soon as they are spoken we know them as our own. (Malouf in White, 2000, p. 145)

White goes on to highlight that what particularly spoke to him from this segment was the idea of 'little sacraments of daily existence', which he suggests reminds us to be open to those little events in people's lives that can evoke a sense of the significant or of the sacred. He points out that these little everyday kinds of occurrences can often be overlooked, perhaps because they are the sort of events that mainstream culture does not particularly value. I will return later to this idea of finding words for our experiences.

This state of curiosity about those other little events in people's lives that can suggest significance and draw our attention to aspects of their lives that are meaningful but have previously been overlooked and un-storied is part of the philosophical stance that is useful for developing narrative practices. This stance may encourage us to listen for and notice those events that might be re-authored into a preferred storyline, as described in Chapter 1.

White's comments also remind me of the first description of Celtic spirituality I heard, which was from a member of the Sisters of St John the Divine Anglican (Church of England) Community. She explained to me that the Celts believed in the intertwining of the sacred and mystical within the physical, so that the spiritual world was believed to be all around and close at hand. She suggested that for the Celts it was not necessary to stop to kneel and to pray to a God 'out there', but that they would be able to engage with the Divine through their day-to-day activities, like putting on the kettle or sweeping the hearth. This description leads me to think of all the tangible ways in which parents show one another and their children that they love them: not by simply saying the words, but by how they act on a daily basis, which may not be rewarded by the goal-directed discourses of society, but may be what matters most to people. White's comments suggest that our professional activities can also support and highlight the importance, perhaps the sacredness, of these everyday activities.

I will come back to the possibilities available through engaging with what Celtic spirituality might have to offer us in thinking about how to integrate spirituality into practice.

Changes in spirituality and mental health

As Sims and Cook (in Cook, Powell & Sims, 2009) comment, despite the care of people having historically been provided within a spiritual or religious context, the split between religion, spirituality and matters related to the care of the physical and mental health of people became grounded in scientific rationality and material realism by the middle of the twentieth century. They note that Freud's assertion that belief in a God was delusional put psychoanalysis, and therefore psychiatry, in conflict with religious attitudes and beliefs. Although in the 1960s there was no sense that the patient's religious beliefs or spirituality contributed significantly to the psychiatric history, assessment or treatment plan, they point out that 'research in the area of mental illness and religious belief developed during the 1990s from almost none to an accepted area of enquiry with research funding' (p. 4).

Drawing on research studies, Sims and Cook are able to conclude that spirituality and religion are able to contribute the following:

1. Promote a positive worldview.
2. Help to make sense of difficult situations.
3. Give purpose and meaning.
4. Discourage maladaptive coping.
5. Enhance social support.
6. Promote 'other-directedness'.
7. Help to release the need for control.
8. Provide and encourage forgiveness.
9. Encourage thankfulness.
10. Provide hope. (Cook, Powell & Sims, 2009, p. 10)

Despite the fact that there is now research that supports the importance of spirituality in people's lives, Sims and Cook continue to propose that further thought and training have to be devoted to how the area of spirituality is best introduced into the bio-psychosocial assessments of professional practice. Although they suggest that at times it may be useful to ask people specifically what they think about whether spirituality may or may not have played a role in the development of their problems and possible solutions, given the broad definition of spirituality it is important to address more broadly what gives people a sense of meaning and hope, in order to assist them in becoming clearer about their beliefs and commitments and thus better able to make choices about preferred ways of being.

Celtic spirituality, nature and the everyday

Returning to the area of Celtic spirituality, it is possible to consider how it may offer us ways of thinking further about the little sacraments of daily living, privileging further those day-to-day activities that are important to the people with whom we meet, and also provide ideas about the sacred within the physical environment.

Davies and O'Loughlin (1999) point out that for academics there is some difficulty in pinpointing and defining 'the Celts', 'spirituality' and, therefore, 'Celtic spirituality', but that nevertheless there is a common consensus of what is implied by these terms. They state that although potentially misleading, 'Celtic' remains a useful term, and refers to those cultures along the western fringe of the British Isles and particularly Wales and Ireland. They also maintain that Christian spirituality as it developed within these Celtic cultures in early medieval times can be characterized in the following manner:

> Particularly in vernacular sources, nature appears as a theme to an unusual degree, and enjoys its own autonomy, rather than purely serving the human ends of atmosphere and mood as an imitation of the classical mise-en-scène. Human creativity is drawn to the center of the Christian life in Irish art and Welsh poetry, both of which stress the role of imagination … But we also find here a wonderfully life-affirming and exuberant kind of Christianity that must owe something of its spirit to pre-Christian forms of religious life among the Celts. The relative innocence and freshness of early Celtic Christianity is a discovery that the modern observer, wearied by the abstractions and dualisms of body in opposition to spirit that have dogged the Christian tradition in its more classical forms, may find welcome. (Davies & O'Loughlin, 1999, pp. 11–12)

Bradley (2010) also describes Celtic spirituality and its appeal to people today. He says, 'For the Celts, God was to be found, and worshipped, as much in the little everyday tasks of life as in the great cosmic dramas like the dance of the sun at Easter time' (p. 39). He goes on:

> Instinctively too they knew what sociologists and psychologists are increasingly telling us – that ritual and ceremony, investing even the simplest and most commonplace tasks and events with a sense of worth and a measure of transcendence, is vital to the health of both societies and individuals. One of the most important practical lessons that we can learn from the Celts is to reinvest, to value again the importance of the

little things and to find God once more in the trivial round and the common task. (Bradley, 2010, p. 39)

Eco-spirituality and person-as-place

It was due to my interest in mindfulness (Béres, 2009), as well as in spirituality within narrative and social work practice, that I began a research project in 2010 that involved travelling in Ireland, Scotland, Wales and England, visiting sites that have been described as sacred and spiritual. This project started with a week-long stay on the island of Iona in the Inner Scottish Hebrides. Pilgrims and tourists visit Iona primarily because of its connection to St Columba and a radical ecumenical organization called the 'Iona Community' that runs programmes in the rebuilt Benedictine monastery on the island. Iona has been called the 'cradle of Christianity in Scotland' (MacArthur, 2007, p. 9), due to the fact that Columba arrived there from Ireland in 563 CE (Bradley, 2009, p. 120) and set up a monastery, which became the centre of early Christian influence in the British Isles. Scholars of Celtic spirituality write of the impact of Columba and his monks on the integration of pagan and Christian beliefs in what we now refer to as Ireland, Scotland, Wales, England and France.

I have previously written about my interest in Celtic spirituality and about interviews I conducted with people concerning their engagement with physical place (Béres, 2012, 2013). What I want to focus on here, however, is what people said in research interviews about the importance of physical place and their experiences of meaning-making, linking their insights to a growing body of literature regarding eco-spirituality and 'person-as-place'.

I conducted 17 in-depth interviews between June and November of 2010. I interviewed four Canadians, three English people, three Irish and five Scottish people, and two further interviewees who were originally from the United States but were living in Scotland at the time of the interview. Seven of the people were men and ten women. Five identified themselves as not having a religious affiliation and not thinking of themselves usually as being particularly spiritual, but nonetheless they provided interesting accounts of a sense of meaning and purpose they had experienced due to their engagement with certain physical places. Of the other twelve, one identified as having left the Roman Catholic priesthood in order to become a Celtic monk, five were active in Church of England/Anglican churches and the other six were involved in Roman Catholic congregations. Although one of the women I interviewed indicated she had been a practising Buddhist for a short period, she had returned to the Church of England for her worship and sense of community when I met her.

On my first visit to Iona in June 2010, I had not previously read anything about Celtic spirituality, but had been told that Iona has been described by many as a 'thin place'. George MacLeod is claimed to have been the first to describe Iona in this way (Bentley & Paynter, 2011, p. 7). In doing so he was drawing on descriptions of how the Celts experienced 'the narrowness of the line that divides this world from the next. This intertwining of the natural and the supernatural, the material and spiritual was carried over when they became Christians' (Bradley, 2010, p. 37).

Over the course of a year I visited Iona on three different occasions, incorporating in these trips visits to other sites of Celtic influence, and I also began studying Celtic spirituality. Fr Frank Fahey, whom I interviewed at Ballintubber Abbey in Ireland and who has been integrating Celtic spirituality into his Roman Catholic faith and practice for the past 40 years, presented an opposing argument to that implied by George MacLeod's contention that Iona is a 'thin place'. Fahey suggests, more in keeping with Celtic theology's notion of 'God is close' (O'Loghlin, 2000, p. 333), that the boundary between the physical world and the spiritual world is thin everywhere, not only in certain special places. North American and Australian Aboriginal spirituality also considers the physical environment as sacred (Berry, 1988; Crisp, 2010; Zapf, 2007, 2010).

Crisp (2010), in discussing her very general description of spirituality as being what gives people a sense of purpose, belonging or meaning, describes stages of spirituality and suggests that for teens, music and coming together with friends at clubs are meaningful. Communing with nature probably would not be as meaningful to a teen who finds meaning at raves.

In describing how people of different ages respond to the crisis of environmental decline, Lysack (2010) points out that 'our sense of loss appears to be experienced differently, depending on the developmental life-cycle stage of the individual' (p. 50). Just as spirituality will be experienced differently at different ages, he gives examples of how concerns for the environment and eco-spirituality will be experienced differently at different ages and stages. He suggests, for example, that primary school children will most likely be concerned for particular physical aspects, like rivers, or specific animals. He mentions that 'bears, turtles, and wolves figure prominently' (p. 50). He goes on to describe how as children's cognitive functioning and moral perspectives develop, they are more apt to place their concerns in a broader context. By the age of 9, children might ask why degradation and extinction occur and teenagers might start focusing on advocacy, social justice and concrete action, like habitat restoration.

Approximately 20 years ago I met a monk who told me that he thought the power of pilgrimages had to do with the fact that they require people to leave home and experience totally different cultures and communities. He felt that in returning from pilgrimages it was impossible for people ever again to think that their way was the only way of doing things, so a pilgrimage forces people to reflect on 'taken-for-granteds': those things that had previously been almost invisible because they were simply part of everyday life. This may assist people in developing a greater sense of humility, recognizing that things do not have to be done the way they have always done them and recognizing the beauty and creativity of other people and cultures. What I have found, however, is that having been to Iona and having appreciated what could be described as a relatively stark kind of beauty, and having allowed myself the time and space to slow down and appreciate the beauty of, for example, a watery sun in a cold, grey winter sky in Iona, my eyes have opened up to a similar type of beauty at home. I was embarrassingly surprised after returning from Iona in November 2010 to realize that I could look at the same winter sky and sun in Canada and recognize it as beautiful when I had not previously really noticed or appreciated it. This could be described as noticing something I had previously taken for granted in my everyday activities, perhaps noticing the sacred within the physical, and exoticizing the domestic.

In November 2010, I also visited Aberdeen in Scotland and facilitated a focus group with five people who had been identified through word of mouth from another woman who had been willing to be interviewed for my project in June that year. Two of the participants were married to one another and were originally from the United States. The other three were all originally from Scotland, but appeared to have travelled extensively. None of them identified finding organized religion or formal religious buildings as particularly meaningful, but they were all interested in thinking and talking about the connection between spirituality and physical places, and willing to describe memories of times when they had experienced a sense of something spiritual. They all provided me with consent to describe their experiences.

Sandra shared a couple of memories of moments in nature when she said she experienced a profound sense of joy, which she described as ecstasy. The first was when she was 12 years old and was riding her pony on her parents' farm. She said that she usually resented the isolation of living on a farm and was generally quite pragmatic and unlikely to think in spiritual terms. On the day she recalled, she said that she was riding her pony on the edge of the farm property fairly early in the morning when the sun had a particular golden hue to it and she was suddenly completely overwhelmed with joy. She said that she had not really thought much in terms of God, but at that moment she felt grateful to God and to her parents for giving her the kind of life in which she could have a pony and experience this connection with nature. She said that she had a similarly profound experience of ecstasy when she was 26 and living in South Africa. She was running on the beach by herself and was overwhelmed by how fantastic it was, how lucky she was, and again how joyful this was. She added that she was not spiritual at the time, but she thinks back on the experience now as having been spiritual.

Both Sandra and Andrea mentioned how they are often drawn to spend time at the sea, and that this could be in the warm waters of the Mediterranean, but could just as easily be on the east coast of Scotland in the cold winter months, merely looking out to sea. Sandra said that looking out to sea after a day of stress can result in the stress 'falling off her shoulders like a cloak sliding off'. Andrea and Bruce both mentioned the act of cycling and something about the methodical rhythm of cycling being like a meditation, but also the relief of getting out of Aberdeen on bicycles and into the countryside as another antidote to the stress of their lives in the city.

Carrie spoke of meeting with a spiritual director when she was attending university in the United States and how tiny and crammed her spiritual director's office was. 'However,' she said, 'because of what we talked about, the space ended up feeling huge and open, because I could be free there and there was a sense of spaciousness.' In a similar vein, reflecting on places that had been unexpectedly spiritual, Bruce mentioned 'aha moments' at a Starbucks coffee shop and Andrea talked about the local psychiatric hospital and her Al-Anon group. She said that even if when she visited the psychiatric hospital there was a lock-down with police involved due to a disturbance on the forensic unit, she always felt safe there. She added that the same was true of her time in Al-Anon meetings and suggested that this was possibly because of the commitment to confidentiality and people's interest in 'connecting to your heart'.

All the comments made in the focus group, whether described here or not, indicated the significance of engagement with various places. These final comments also add encouragement to those of us working in challenging settings that a sense of caring and safety can be provided to people, despite the location, so that they feel a connection being made to their hearts.

Anne, whom I had interviewed in Iona the week before and who lives in Edinburgh, also had drawn my attention to the necessity of a sense of spaciousness, which is interesting given Carrie's description of the feeling of spaciousness in an office because of what was being discussed. Anne's description of spaciousness, on the other hand, came about when she had been standing on a hill at St Columba's Bay on the south shore of Iona, watching a rain system move in. She described this as a moment of feeling both a connection to the physical place and yet also a great sense of spaciousness. She went on to describe this sense of spaciousness as then facilitating further reflections and contemplation while on retreat on Iona.

She said that she lives a quiet and contemplative life at home, does not have a television and turns her phone off at 9 p.m. each night in order to maintain some quiet and peace in her life, and yet life still becomes busy and she finds she needs times of retreat in order to experience spaciousness again.

I wonder what we can do to ensure a growing sense of spaciousness in our conversations, in our offices and on home visits, to provide people with the space to think differently. I think that narrative practices provide many of the specific steps useful in assisting people in reflecting on their personal values, preferences, hopes and meaning-making, yet we may need to think more about how to ensure that extra element of care and connection and not assume that it will simply happen naturally. On the other hand, the process of stepping back and away from the problem storyline, and assisting people in looking for previously un-storied events in their lives, perhaps could be considered as a method for creating a distance from the problem that allows for this sense of space and possibility. Issues of hospitality, which I will address later in this chapter, may offer some further ideas.

As Holloway and Moss (2010) point out, there has been a growing interest in an eco-spiritual perspective and exploration of the importance of '"place" in communal and individual human existence, most especially around questions of identity' (p. 159). Besthorn[1] (2012), Coates (2007), Zapf (2010) and Lysack (2010) are all particularly strong voices in the debates that encourage us to reflect further on how to respond to environmental issues within social work. Holloway and Moss (2010) suggest two implications in particular for social work practice:

> First, the question about the extent to which people have learned, and are still learning, 'how to live well' in their present setting and context is an important issue for us as social workers to look and listen for in our dealings with people. For some people, issues around material prosperity may feature less highly than being able to enjoy and emotionally benefit from a sense of community, where people feel they belong, have a role to play and are cared for by friends and neighbours. … Secondly, but antithetically, the extent to which people feel uprooted, unsettled and unable to live well in their immediate setting and context is equally crucial, not least because the sense of loss and grief that accompanies such experiences of dislocation can be profoundly disabling and dispiriting. (Holloway & Moss, 2010, p. 160)

They go on to point out how this dislocation can be particularly clear when working with immigrant and refugee populations. In fact, Falicov (2007), describing work with transnational immigrants and people with connections across borders, suggests that such people have had to cope with broken hearts as they have felt split between countries. She proposes that when working with this group of people our focus needs to be in relation to assisting people in moving from having a broken heart to having two hearts, as they straddle borders and cope with transnational experiences. She quotes Pavese as saying, 'Having a country means not to be alone, to know that in the people, the plants, the soil, there is something of yours, that even if you are not there, it keeps on waiting for you' (Pavese in Falicov, 2007, p. 157).

Lysack (2010) suggests that asking about emotional connections to physical places can be one step in community education programmes designed to develop a greater awareness of environmental crisis and possible responses. Lysack, like Besthorn and Coates, suggests that social work needs to think through how to integrate ideas of stewardship and care for the world into our practice. He points out that proposing that we should look after the world, and even instilling a sense of the value of the world, does not automatically result in people being willing to look after the environment. He quotes Berry as saying, 'We know enough of our history by now to be aware that people *exploit* what they have merely concluded to be of value, but *defend* what they love' (Berry in Lysack, 2010, p. 56). Coates suggests that the values and beliefs inherent in modernism have led to ecological and human exploitation based on seeing nature as 'other' and 'the tendency to treat all things, both human and non-human, as commodities' (Coates, 2007, p. 216). Moving away from the dualistic thinking as Coates recommends, since it underpins thinking of nature as 'other', is certainly consistent with both post-modern narrative practices and also Celtic spirituality's focus on the divine spark within all of creation, connecting us with creation. This results in a sense of stewardship and care for what is sacred, but perhaps moves us beyond stewardship if we see the interconnectedness instead of dualism. Also drawing on Berry, as well as Kenyon and Randall, Coates goes on to suggest that if 'ecological and social justice are to be attained, humanity requires ... a "new story," perhaps even a "radical re-storying" ... that can eliminate the dualism and exploitation inherent in modern society' (Coates, 2007, p. 217).

Zapf (2010) takes this notion of moving away from dualisms further when he suggests that social work's tradition of focusing on the person in the environment has been insufficient and has resulted in an ever-growing interest in the person and disregard for the context of the environment. Having been influenced by his work with rural and Aboriginal communities, Zapf has also reflected on the importance of place in people's lives. He suggests that we consider 'place' rather than 'environment', and even that we should consider the metaphor of 'people as place' rather than 'people in place' or even 'people with place'. He presents his argument clearly:

Human health and welfare is bound up with environmental health and welfare. Environments are not merely lifeless backdrops for human activity, any more than people are merely temporary actors in an ongoing natural system. We are entwined with the natural world in a continuing process of co-creation. Human development cannot be separated from stewardship of the earth. In short, we are our surroundings; *people as place*. (Zapf, 2010, p. 39)

Besthorn (2012) reviews the contributions of deep ecology to social work over the past ten years, also suggesting that responsible stewardship of the Earth is required and is a necessary element of social work practice, since social work is concerned with the well-being and survival of people. Also consistent with Coates, he says that modern societies need to shift away from their obsession with consumerism, and rather focus on the quality of living in place. He says, 'attachment to place – and of fully existing in the natural and built forms humans inhabit – has been a central, if sometimes misunderstood, feature of Deep Ecology' (p. 253). He goes on to explain that it has been important to many supporters of deep ecology to design built places that incorporate natural places, focusing on eco-friendly architecture and planning. He explains that deep ecology and a respect for the natural environment do not require a preoccupation with wilderness or a return to the wilderness, but rather a commitment to 'finding a balance between wild and built nature' (p. 254).

I have a great deal of respect for these writers I have mentioned who are raising concerns about the environmental crisis and the need to teach and advocate for changes in how many mainstream societies think about physical place and human interaction with the non-human environment. I agree with Lysack, however, that a rational argument for why this is important does not always go very far, and that people need to experience an emotional connection to a physical place before they will begin to think about making changes in how they live. What I have found missing from much of their writing is a description of how to integrate these concerns into our practice with individuals, since so much of social work practice is about working with individuals and families. Their arguments tend to suggest that social work has focused too much on the individual and, therefore, they do not give us suggestions for incorporating their reflections into work with individuals.

I am hoping that by reviewing these ideas about spirituality and place within this book regarding narrative practices with people, I will be sparking an interest in practitioners to begin integrating people's meaning-making and engagement with place as forms of spirituality that are crucial. This does not mean that we should impose our ideas about spirituality, since counselling is not, and should not be, about proselytizing. As Lysack (2010) points out, however, people often experience reactions that seem outside the realm of language, that suddenly seem to leap forward and take shape, if we are able to ask the questions that will help people change their relationships with their experiences. This description shares much in common with the process of re-authoring through assisting people in reclaiming events in their past that have previously been un-storied. It provides the necessary language and structure for people to make meaning of their experiences, but, given the social construction involved in our conversations, it is up to us to be curious about all these various elements of a person's life if these experiences are to have a chance to come forward.

Spirituality and hospitality in practice

Within the context of considering definitions of spirituality and ways of opening up space for discussions of spirituality in practice, it was interesting to hear David Epston (2012) suggest that it might be time to remind ourselves as practitioners in health and social services of the art and ethics of hospitality. Although the word 'hospitality' might now make some people think of 'hospitality services' and the training and management of hotel staff, he reminded us that 'hospitality' derives from the same root word as 'hospice' and 'hospital' and was in fact an important aspect of Benedictine monasteries. Hospitality, therefore, also has a link to spirituality and an ethics of care.

Chittister (2004[1994]), in her commentary on the Rule of Benedict, describes what the Benedictine tradition had to say about guests and hospitality and what we can learn from this tradition for our lives today. Although Benedictine monasteries were set up for monks to be able to pray and work separated from the distractions of the rest of the world, they were also places where they were to receive guests. Chittister says that the monks were in fact instructed to consider hospitality as one form of worship: 'The message to the stranger is clear: Come right in and disturb our perfect lives. You are the Christ for us today' (pp. 140–41). She goes on to add that a guest was, and should also now be, received without judging whether we like the person or are impressed with the person's appearance and accomplishments:

> In Benedictine spirituality, too, hospitality is clearly meant to be more than an open door. It is an acknowledgement of the gifts the stranger brings ... But Benedictine hospitality is also a return of gifts. The stranger is shown both presence and service ... Benedictine hospitality is the gift of one human being to another. (Chittester, 2004[1994], pp. 141–2)

Just as I described the ethics of care in Chapter 1 as not necessarily flowing from professional codes of ethics, this notion of hospitality also suggests basic good manners and politeness, which have more in common with a feminist ethics of care than they do with professional standards of practice. Parton (2003) highlights how social work, when it is practised in traditional *professional* manners, can in fact be experienced by service users as formal, adversarial and expert driven with imposed resolutions. He suggests that by examining the contributions of a feminist ethics of care, which share much more in common with post-modern and social constructionist approaches to practice, we can move towards a connected and relationship-based practice, resulting in cooperation, explorations of possibilities, expectations of possible change, stronger bonds and personal renewal.

Aristarkhova (2012) has taken the concept of hospitality as usually described by Levinas and Derrida and has suggested that feminists take up the concept and show the link between hospitality and the maternal. She describes how Levinas and Derrida were influenced by Jewish and Christian accounts of hospitality, and how they particularly struggled with understanding how individuals and communities could welcome strangers/'Others' against the backdrop of the challenges and horrors of the Holocaust. She says, 'it is important to stress that hospitality is introduced in Derrida as a radical concept that tries to open up other possibilities for treating others and therefore as a movement beyond tolerance' (p. 167). The strength of Aristarkhova's arguments is in her presentation of the concepts that Levinas and Derrida suggest, yet I am less convinced by her suggestions that femininity and the maternal are natural forms of hospitality. I prefer Parton's advice:

> It is being argued that it is important not to see elements of difference simply in terms of an essentialist binary of opposites. Rather than see established rationality as being in opposition to the emotions, it is now being argued that it is vital to see the emotions as central to everyone; it is not a parochial concern of women alone. For example, care receiving makes one aware of one's vulnerability and vulnerability is not only an issue for children and elders, but is something which we all – at different times and in different ways – experience. It thus has clear implications for the way we think about social work and the way it is experienced and organized. (Parton, 2003, p. 11)

Aman (2006) has written a short description of the 'therapist as host', due to remarks made by Epston in a training session she attended. She suggests that his remarks resonated for her, and she has described how she integrated them with reflections she had been having about the role of hospitality and care as demonstrated in her grandmother's life through her actions towards others. Since Aman is a private practitioner in the United States, her comments are primarily in terms of how to make her counselling office a warm and welcoming space, and how to market her practice and then engage in conversation and in writing with people in such a way as to demonstrate this welcoming manner. Nonetheless, it is interesting to read that she has also been inspired by these ideas of hospitality in practice and the practitioner as host. In addition to thinking of ourselves as hosts, I would suggest that when we are conducting home visits, we might actually need also to think about how to be a good, respectful guest rather than a host.

As Aristarkhova (2012) indicates, hosting suggests that we own the property into which we welcome a guest; and the ownership and ability to choose intentionally to welcome someone imply power over the guest. This description is certainly consistent with the situation in which practitioners find themselves with people who request services. Although we may wish to make the person feel welcome and part of a collaborative process, we cannot ignore the fact that we have more power and that we are challenged to use that power ethically. I suggest that one way of using our power ethically and in a manner that will be experienced as more respectful and collaborative is to think through how we can learn from the discourses of hospitality in our hosting skills and in our behaviours, as we are sometimes required to take up positions as unwelcome guests on home visits.

Although Levinas (in Aristarkhova, 2012) suggests particular elements of hospitality – welcome, intentionality, receptivity, discretion, intimacy, recollection and habitation – it is probably also useful to reflect on what elements you have found that have contributed to your sense of having been offered hospitality, and also to ask those people with whom you have worked what has helped them experience a sense of hospitality. It is, of course, quite possible that different people will require different elements in order to feel welcomed and respected and ready to work within a context of hospitality. A 'host' may have the best of intentions in telling a guest to make herself at home and then respecting her to leave her to fend for herself, but many guests could feel ignored and disrespected through this approach. Most guests will benefit from, and appreciate, care and attention that indicate a true interest in them and concern for their comfort and well-being.

Focusing on attempts to integrate ideas of hosting and hospitality may also suggest moving away from discourses of 'interviewing' and towards discourses of 'conversations'. This has had an impact on the language used in narrative practice conferences; for example, the series of 'Therapeutic Conversations' conferences organized in North America, and the language used in writing when authors use the word 'people' instead of 'clients' and 'service users'. As Epston has suggested (2012), taking up a conversational and hospitable stance also has an effect on how we ask questions and demonstrate curiosity. He has been focusing in recent training contexts on assisting participants in developing the kinds of skills that invite people to become ever more curious about their own lives, and engage them in recounting rich and detailed narratives of what has been important to them.

What I was reminded of by Epston, in the most recent training I attended, was the importance of *inviting* people to tell us about themselves, rather than asking them very direct questions, and of being *curious* about the details of their stories so that they can embroider the series of events with the taste and feel of the experiences they are recounting. In order to have us practise and develop the skills further in asking these types of questions, we engaged in very slow-paced conversations, stopping and starting and developing two or three different questions from which a person could choose the one to answer. Together we reflected on why certain questions were more invitational and interesting than others, and why people chose to respond to those questions rather than others. This is an activity in which a group of practitioners could engage if they wished to consult and practise developing narrative styles of conversations.

> **Practice example**
>
> I invited Melissa[2] to contribute a practice example from her work with refugees to demonstrate the way in which she incorporates a respect for spirituality into her practice. She speaks Spanish, as well as English, fluently, and is therefore often able to respond to requests for services for Spanish-speaking refugees. Although practitioners in the United Kingdom are likely to work with refugees from different parts of the world than practitioners in Canada, I believe that the ideas Melissa presents will be relevant and transferable. She has offered the following example:

> **Case study**
>
> It is with deep gratitude and the awareness of much privilege that I engage with refugees in crafting letters of assessment and advocacy to support their immigration cases, as well as in ongoing therapeutic support to cope with the effects of trauma, and to make meaning of their new life in Canada. The refugees with whom I am in contact are predominantly representative of

countries in Central and South America where widespread gang and paramilitary violence flourishes without consequence. It is almost exclusively for reasons of violence, or threat of imminent violence, that these refugees flee their home countries.

Sandra was one such refugee: a young woman of 21 years of age from El Salvador, the Central American country known as the forerunner for gang violence by the infamous MS-13 and 18th Street gangs. It was the 18th Street gang that would change Sandra's life as she knew it for ever. It is commonly known in Central America that some of the tactics of fear and intimidation utilized by gangs are to extort and to kidnap for the purposes of ransoms, forced recruitment of youth into the gangs and, with women, sexual exploitation.

Sandra's parents were young when Sandra's mother became pregnant and her father left because he did not want a child. Sandra lived with, and was raised by, both her mother and her maternal grandparents. Her grandfather died when she was a young girl and her mother died of cancer early in Sandra's teen years. From that point on, Sandra and her grandmother were left to fend for themselves with no other family close by. Sandra was thankful that there was a sizeable amount of money to support her and her grandmother from her grandfather's savings, as he had been a successful and well-known businessman during his career. Sandra expressed how protective she felt of her grandmother and that she worked very hard to care for her.

Despite all of the tragedy Sandra had already experienced in her young life, she had a strong drive to make her mother, grandmother and grandfather proud of her by pursuing her hopes and dreams with perseverance, as they had always encouraged. However, as a young woman, early on in her post-secondary education with aspirations of nursing, Sandra had a violent encounter with the 18th Street gang on her walk home from university that changed the course of her life.

Sandra was kidnapped, sexually assaulted and then released with threats of extortion for her grandfather's money. In subsequent days, Sandra and her grandmother received phone calls demanding specific amounts of money and threats. It quickly became evident that both of them were in grave and imminent danger. Much to Sandra's protest, her grandmother insisted that she flee the country immediately. Sandra's grandmother was not in the health or physical condition to go with Sandra, but had decided that she would find safe haven at a distant relative's home on the other side of El Salvador; her primary concern was for Sandra's safety and she wanted Sandra to find a new home where she could flourish and follow through with her life dreams.

Sandra made the harrowing journey via people smugglers on foot and by jumping on trains all the way from El Salvador, across the Rio Grande in Mexico, through the desert into the United States and finally up to Canada. Along the way Sandra experienced harm from the people smuggling her.

Sandra and I began working together at a time when she was dealing with multiple manifestations of post-traumatic stress. She had just been forced to flee her country and was now in a completely unfamiliar place, trying to get by with the limited English she spoke, feeling overwhelmed and fearful of the outcome of her immigration process, not only for her own well-being but also for that of her grandmother.

During my work with Sandra, there were a number of aspects of narrative therapy that were particularly helpful, such as the philosophy of de-centring myself as 'expert' in order to create an emotionally safe and non-judgemental space where she could share her stories in a way that gave her the power to make meaning of her experiences. This was especially helpful for Sandra, as she later identified that from her experience, Latin culture typically fosters a mentality of deferring to authority without question. From early on in our work, I was quite aware of how easy it could be to become mired in the trauma storyline, and so it was initially a challenge to integrate dialogue outside of the problem storyline, which is what we first had to focus on in order to collect information for the Immigration Board. However, as my work with Sandra was not as time limited as in some situations, our work progressed beyond the immigration letter and I was able to discuss with Sandra aspects of herself and her life experiences that were not part of the trauma story. Each time we engaged in this kind of dialogue, it inevitably produced a palpable difference in Sandra's affective expression, tone of voice and body posture. I found it a helpful entry point to open dialogue with Sandra around the things she was particularly fond of about her home country: aspects she felt the world needed to know beyond the typically negative news reports.

Sandra's love for her home country, her cultural roots and her family and friends were poignantly evident when I asked her about a particular place that might come to mind for her that would best describe where she had felt safety, peace and/or tranquillity. She was able to recall a favourite location in her family home, the kitchen, connected by a walkway out to the backyard, which overlooked a lush area of land that was her family's property. When I asked about the details of the space, Sandra, engaging description through all the senses, described the place in meticulous detail. She spoke of the memories made in that kitchen; cooking skills passed down to her by her grandmother; dancing with her grandfather to their favourite cultural music; and supportive talks with her mother about life. She also spoke of the lush land that was the family property, how much she enjoyed learning about the different plants and flowers her grandmother tended every year, and the tranquillity and comfort she found there amid a rich natural world. We discussed what Sandra might call this special place if she were to give it a name and she called it 'tranquillity'. I asked her if she were to entertain the idea of holding the essence of this place, 'tranquillity', close to her, what that might look like in her everyday life. Sandra said that she felt it helped her in moments of feeling overwhelmed with her situation and distressed by post-traumatic stressors to hold close the love of her mother and grandparents and their encouragement always to persevere and follow her dreams. This led us into some powerful re-membering conversations.

In those re-membering conversations I was able to support Sandra in both maintaining the deep bonds and connections with family members and friends from whom she was separated as well as developing new memberships with people she was encountering in her new life in Canada. These new friendships were clearly not to be a replacement, but rather a new addition of support and connectedness. Sandra experienced a period in which she isolated and disconnected herself from the world because of suspicion and fear, which is common for people who have experienced trauma. I was able to ask after the things that Sandra's mother and grandparents saw in her; things that others might not have known to be true of her; things that they appreciated about her. I also asked her what she thought they might say to her now in her current situation. Making connections through these re-membering conversations proved to act as an important form of resistance for Sandra in light of the potentially devastating effects of trauma and assisted her in moving beyond isolation.

I also found a re-authoring conversation with Sandra to be particularly helpful when discussing the maintenance of cultural identity amid the pull to 'assimilate'. These conversations opened up the space for her to touch on issues related to spirituality. Although Canada prides itself on being a multi-cultural mosaic, Sandra had a number of experiences of oppression early on in her time there. For her, cultural identity was intimately connected with a sense of self, purpose and meaning in a spiritual sense: the sacredness of traditional practices, wisdom, food and music that were also a significant connection with her mother and grandparents. In our re-authoring conversation, Sandra was able to make meaning of her life in all of its newness in Canada as a refugee, as well as maintaining and upholding her own cultural values and ways of being.

Another key aspect of our re-authoring conversation had to do with Sandra's Christian faith. She described a crisis of faith in how to understand her experiences in light of her belief that there is a Divine being who wants the best for her life. Sandra was able to process her doubts, questions and confusion and to re-connect with aspects of faith that she was still deeply drawn to, with an even richer understanding of herself and her relationship with the being she referred to as God. Sandra's faith became another key protective factor, a resilience if you will, for her sense of purpose in life, what she referred to as God's purpose for her life, and gratitude for what she described as God's provision in the commonly used phrase 'gracias a Dios', thanks be to God, that she often said.

Sandra and I were also able to engage in an externalizing conversation to grapple with her intense feelings of fear surrounding her experiences of trauma, the safety and well-being of her grandmother and the unknown elements of her immigration process. During our externalizing conversation, Sandra was able specifically to identify the fear, in the form of nightmares about her kidnapping experience and the phone calls received after that incident, that the El Salvadorian gang would eventually find her grandmother and kill her, and that she herself would be denied refugee status, which would not only mean having to return to the dangers of her home country, but also the inability to bring her grandmother to Canada. Sandra was able to recognize that this fear often immobilized her, making it difficult to leave her apartment, difficult to concentrate in her English as a Second Language classes, and difficult to engage in any of the coping strategies and activities that she found life-giving for her at that moment in time. I saw the significant difference for Sandra in her overall quality of life when she was able to identify the effects of fear as detrimental, and then when she came to an understanding of how she felt she could stand up to the fear, in both her thoughts and her actions.

Because Sandra was without the option of returning to her home country for obvious safety reasons, it was critical to create a safe, supportive space where she could tell and re-tell her stories in a way that brought about new meaning-making beyond trauma, fear and suffering, and to re-claim a sense of connection with her homeland and her family.

Melissa's description of her work with Sandra provides another example of how the various conversation maps fit together to support movement towards a person's alternative storyline and way of being in the world, in addition to the examples I presented in Chapter 4. Sandra may have preferred, if it were a perfect world, to be back in El Salvador if she could have been there safely. This description, therefore, also provides a practice example of working with a person where the alternative, or preferred, story-line towards which she moves may be the one that she believes is best, given the current circumstances; preferred storylines are not unrealistic. Finally, Melissa's description of her work with Sandra also provides a glimpse of how issues regarding place and spirituality can be integrated smoothly into conversations, opening up the space for re-connecting to aspects of life that have been rich with meaning.

Conclusion

I have touched briefly in this chapter on many aspects related to spirituality and practice. Spirituality, as an aspect of meaning-making and purpose in people's lives, is a vital aspect of social work and counselling. As Holloway (2007) has indicated, society may currently be described as less religious and more secular, but the majority of people continue to describe themselves as believing in 'some sort of God, or greater power' (p. 266). She goes on to report that 'there is recognition of the growing popularity of "new-age" practices and the permeation of more diffuse spirituality, as well as revived interest in traditional forms as Celtic spirituality' (p. 266). Rather than practitioners becoming caught up in concerns about religion, it may be more useful to focus on what those people in conversation with us have to say about what gives them meaning and purpose; that may, or may not, involve discussions about organized religion.

I am also excited by the possibilities provided by the growing interest in our spiritual connection to the earth. There is still much to learn, or rather re-learn, as Scharper (2013) puts it: 'this is a moment of retrieval, redeeming, reflecting, a dialectical swirl of reinterpretation for this time' (p. 198). He particularly focuses on the need truly to reconcile authentically with Aboriginal peoples, and learn from their teaching. I agree totally with Scharper and would also comment that a re-connection to ancient Celtic understandings will add to the conversation.

Finally, I have been interested in considering the possibilities inherent in thinking about how discourses of hospitality might assist practitioners in further reflection regarding how to create welcoming and invitational contexts for practice and conversation. I hope that these considerations will be of interest to other practitioners as they think about how to be good guests in other people's homes, as well as how to be welcoming hosts in their own workplaces.

Notes

1. Besthorn has also developed a website, www.ecosocialwork.org, as a site for a global alliance for a deep ecological approach to social work.

2. Melissa Page Nichols, MSW, RSW, is a narrative practitioner and social worker in a campus ministry context. She was previously a student in my Narrative Therapy elective and is now a colleague of mine who attends the narrative consultation group and teaches part time in the social work programme.

8 Notes on Self-Care and the Ongoing Effects of Working as a Narrative Practitioner

Introduction

Foucault, in describing 'the hermeneutic of the subject', points out that as far back as the 400s BCE, philosophers were reflecting on the fact that we must take care of ourselves if we are meant also to attend to others (1994, p. 96). The notion of self-care is often suggested to people working within social and health services; we are told that we need to model appropriate self-care and boundary-setting to people receiving services, and also that we need to look after ourselves so that we do not 'burn out', become worn out or sick and therefore unable to continue caring for others. A continuum of possible negative effects of working in direct services is thought to range from feeling a little fed up and relieved when someone cancels an appointment all the way to vicarious trauma and the need for extended stress leave (Patsiopoulos & Buchanan, 2011; Rothschild, 2006).

I will discuss the topics of self-care and the effects of working with others from a narrative perspective that attempts to unpack the discourses inherent in these concerns. Rather than duplicating mainstream approaches that run the risk of overly focusing on the burdens and potential risks of this work, I will discuss its positive consequences and satisfaction. It is important to take up these issues with a political and social awareness, however, since as Foucault also indicates, 'attending to oneself is a privilege; ... as against those who must attend to others to serve them or attend to a trade in order to live' (1994, p. 95). Finally, I will also include some practical and pragmatic examples of self-care and self-compassion that I, and others, have found useful.

Historical context

Foucault describes the term 'technologies of the self' as 'the procedures, which no doubt exist in every civilization, suggested or prescribed to individuals in order to determine their identity, maintain it, or transform it in terms of a certain number of ends, through relations of self-mastery or self-knowledge' (1994, p. 87). He pursues his interest in the history of subjectivity by exploring the history of self-care and the techniques of the government of the self. He suggests that, despite the difficulties in pinpointing a particular moment in which the focus on self-care emerged, an extensive interest in reflecting on modes of living and regulations of the self developed in the Hellenistic and Roman period (p. 89).[1]

Foucault provides a fascinating account of the shifts in focus on self-care through Western[2] history, starting with Plato's *Alcibiades I* in approximately 350 BCE, then describing the use of self-writing and correspondence in the Hellenistic age, and also indicating how deeply rooted this type of technology of the self was by the time Augustine started his *Confessions* in approximately 397 CE (1994, p. 232). In examining the genealogy of self-care, he describes 'four main problems that endure throughout antiquity' (p. 231) that have troubled philosophers, despite different solutions being offered across time. He presents these four problems as:

- The relation between the care of the self and political action.
- The relationship between the care of the self and pedagogy.
- The relationship between the care of the self and the knowledge of oneself.
- The relationship between the care of the self and philosophical love, or relation to a master. (Foucault, 1994, p. 231)

Foucault goes on to suggest that 'the new care of the self involved a new experience of self' (p. 232). As practices supported attention to the details of day-to-day life through the process of writing, 'a whole field of experience opened which earlier was absent' (p. 233). Through his reference to a letter written in 144–45 CE by Marcus Aurelius to Fronto, Foucault points out the interesting relation between body and soul. He says:

> Marcus Aurelius speaks of himself, his health, what he has eaten, his sore throat. That is quite characteristic of the ambiguity about the body in this cultivation of the self. Theoretically, the cultivation of the self is soul-oriented, but all the concerns of the body take on a considerable importance. In Pliny and Seneca, hypochondria is an essential trait. They retreat to a house in the countryside. They have intellectual activities but rural activities as well. They eat and participate in the activities of peasants. The importance of the rural retreat in this letter is that nature helps put one in contact with oneself. (Foucault, 1994, p. 234)

Focusing on self-care is not a new, nor need it be a self-indulgent exercise, but rather a topic that has concerned people for approximately 2400 years.

It is interesting to reflect on the foundation of the unease that some of us might have in discussing self-care: which discourses have, in fact, contributed to thoughts that this might be self-indulgent? Foucault may offer some further possibilities as he traces the shift from pagan to Christian cultures, noting also the differences between Catholic and Reformation traditions (p. 242). Although he points out that 'penance and the confession of sins are rather late innovations' (p. 243), and are quite different from the actions of first-century Christians, public demonstrations of shame and humility continued as main forms of punishment until the fifteenth and sixteenth centuries (p. 244). He suggests that this theme of self-renunciation (self-denial) is important and is linked within Christianity with the verbal or dramatic disclosure of the self. I wonder whether some of us continue to be influenced by a Protestant work ethic and shame with regard to looking after our physical and emotional needs. Foucault completes his reflections on the technologies of the self by saying:

> From the eighteenth century to the present, the techniques of verbalization have been reinserted in a different context by so-called human sciences in order to use them without renunciation of the self but to constitute, positively, a new self. To use these techniques without renouncing oneself constitutes a decisive break. (Foucault, 1994, p. 249)

Although it is possible to develop an awareness of the technologies of the self and the manners in which we create our identities, the lingering effects of the expectations of self-denial continue to have an influence in those cultures that have been influenced by salvation and confessional religions. This is complex, since there are also many discourses available within these same cultures that suggest immediate gratification in a consumer-driven society. It is not possible to live without the impacts of these various contradictory messages, but each of us can decide our own course for manoeuvring our way through this force field, making our own choices regarding self-care and the formation of our identities.

Working narratively

When asked about how to manage stress, compassion fatigue, secondary trauma or vicarious trauma, my first reaction is to remember comments that Michael White made in a training conference I attended (2006). He suggested that he believed himself to be protected from such things as vicarious trauma because he worked from a narrative approach, with all the philosophical and political positions that this implies. In particular, moving away from a professional position dictated by mainstream notions of expertise can assist in many ways. It encourages a more ethical engagement with people and their stories, since it focuses on assisting people in developing their own courses of action based on their own preferences and values. A side effect of this positive movement towards privileging the insider knowledge of the people consulting us, rather than imposing expert outsider knowledge, is that this frees us from the overwhelming responsibility of having to know how to fix every problem. What works for one person may not make sense for someone else. It is better that we become experts in developing safe relationships in which we listen and ask interesting and useful questions that assist the other people in the conversation to come up with personal and relevant solutions.

My own experience working as a narrative practitioner, and as a social worker engaged in services with women who had experienced childhood sexual abuse and abuse from intimate partners, children who had witnessed domestic violence, and also with men who had perpetrated abuse against their female partners, has been that I have also been spared the experience of secondary or vicarious trauma. Early on in my career as a social worker when I was first beginning to work with adult survivors of childhood sexual abuse, and before I had started fully integrating narrative practices into my approach, I asked my supervisor how she managed to cope with hearing such painful stories of abuse several times each day. I admitted to her that at times I had felt as though I had a weight pushing down on me as I made my way home, while I was still thinking about the details people had shared with me during the day. She wisely told me that she focused on the fact that the women had survived rather than on the fact that they had been abused. Focusing on the fact that someone has survived abuse, how she survived the abuse and that she is continuing to work on moving forward and leaving the pain behind is consistent with narrative re-authoring practices and assists us also in protecting ourselves from the effects of listening to accounts of the abuse. As I have indicated in earlier chapters, this does not mean ignoring the pain and the problem storyline, it means balancing this with also focusing on the other person's resilience, strengths and alternative storylines, which can assist that person to move into preferred ways of being with others.

Vicarious resilience

A relatively new concept referred to as vicarious resilience has been proposed from research conducted by Hernández, Gangsei and Engstrom (2007), which is consistent with the approach my supervisor suggested to me 20 years ago, and also with narrative ideas of balancing the focus on problem storylines with a focus on alternative storylines. Hernández, a counselling psychologist, Gangsei, a clinical psychologist, and Engstrom, a social worker, interviewed 12 practitioners who had worked for between 1 and 18 years in both governmental and non-governmental organizations, providing services to people who had experienced political violence and trauma. Analysing the results of the interviews, they realized that the practitioners not only touched on issues of vicarious trauma, they also highlighted how much they felt they had learnt about resilience from people. They acknowledged that vicarious trauma can negatively affect practitioners working in the field of trauma and can result in anger, fear or frustration. In addition to this, however, they point out that vicarious resilience can be experienced just as much as vicarious trauma if we are reminded to pay attention to it. They go on to describe vicarious resilience as being made up of the following elements:

> Witnessing and reflecting on human beings' immense capacity to heal; reassessing the significance of the therapists' own problems; incorporating spirituality as a valuable dimension in treatment; developing hope and commitment; articulating personal and professional positions regarding political violence; articulating frameworks for healing; developing tolerance to frustration; developing time, setting, and intervention boundaries that fit therapeutic interventions in context; using community interventions; and developing use of self in therapy. (Hernández, Gansei & Engstrom, 2007, p. 238)

Hurley, Martin and Hallberg (2013) have presented the results of a study they conducted in Canada in which they examined how resilience was understood as a concept in child protection practice; what child protection workers did to promote resilience in children and families; and finally, how the child protection workers were affected by the resilience of those children and families. In terms of the effects of resilience on the child protection workers, they found what they called 'a bi-directional "transmission of resilience" in which both people in a relationship are affected by the resilience of the other' (p. 269). They mention one social worker who referred to this as 'a "*contagious process*," meaning that resilience can be triggered by witnessing or participating in the performance of another person's resilience' (p. 269).

Kearns and McArdle (2012) have studied resilience as it is linked to the development of identity in newly qualified social workers in the United Kingdom. They used the Grotberg framework of resilience, made up of 'I am, I have, I can', as a tool to analyse accounts from newly qualified social workers about the construction of their personal (I am), professional (I can) and organizational (I have) identities. Kearns and McArdle point out a frustration with the over-emphasis in the literature nationally and internationally on burnout in the helping professions. They go on to admit that recently there has been a growing interest in the rewards of working in professional practice and that 'several authors now highlight the experience of job satisfaction reported by many social workers despite the demands inherent in the role' (p. 387). Analysis of research participants' accounts indicated the positive significance of reflexivity in the development of self-efficacy, which in turn had a strong connection to the growing sense of self as a social worker. This area straddled the personal and organizational domains, since the quality of peer and supervisory support and consultation was also important for the development of self-efficacy. Kearns and McArdle indicate they were surprised by the low importance of skills, and knowing how to do certain tasks, to the development of resilience and identity construction for these new social workers. They say:

> We were struck rather by the greater emphasis given to reflexive capacity – Most notably, our respondents identify that their growing ability to be reflexive in recognizing, acknowledging to others, and managing the personal investment and emotional demands of the job, has played a key role in their development. (Kearns & McArdle, 2012, p. 391)

One aspect of reflexive practice that they indicate is important is the ability to reframe challenging and uncomfortable situations as opportunities for growth and learning on the journey of becoming a social worker. The journey metaphor certainly shares some commonalities with the narrative metaphor as a series of events are joined across time into a theme; they both have the elements of movement over time and are consistent with the migration of identity metaphor described in Chapter 5. I am not convinced that reflexive practice is a matter of merely reframing an event, however; rather, it is about unpacking all that is inherent in a situation and also looking for other, as yet un-storied, events. Some events might not have anything positive in them, might not have any silver lining, but we might still learn something from them, and we might be able to focus more on the events that are part of our preferred identity and storyline.

A two-way account of therapy

White has made a distinction between one-way and two-way accounts of therapy. In his chapter regarding the therapeutic relationship in *Narratives of Therapists' Lives* (1997), he suggests that a one-way account of therapy is the traditional account that implies a relationship between a 'client' who is in need and a service provider with expert knowledge. The service provider could be trained in any number of different approaches to develop a hypothesis through assessment and then plan interventions depending on their preferred approach. White goes on to point out that although this taken-for-granted account of therapy is mainstream in psychotherapy – and also in social work, I would suggest – plenty of attention is often paid to how problems may arise within this account. Although the expert is there to help the 'client', warnings also abound regarding the dangers of counter-transference, co-dependency and difficulties maintaining boundaries. These are all possible difficulties with which the therapist is required to contend in a one-way account of therapy.

White did not believe that it was possible to work with people in therapy, counselling or social work settings and not be affected by those people, but he did not believe that we had to be affected negatively, as within this one-way account. What he says is consistent with the recent accounts of research regarding vicarious resilience and the construction of our preferred identities. He notes:

> In that the one-way account of therapy structures a relationship to therapeutic practice that disengages us from acts of meaning in relation to those experiences of our work that are potentially shaping of this work, and of our lives, it contributes to thin descriptions of our therapeutic identities, and to thin conclusions about the nature of practice. In stepping into this account of therapy we deny ourselves the opportunity to plot the significant events of our work into the story-lines of our lives. And we deny ourselves that which would otherwise be sustaining of us in the therapeutic endeavour. We become prone to frustration, to fatigue, and to a sense of being burdened by the work. And this ultimately contributes to our vulnerability to experiences of 'burn-out'. (White, 1997, p. 130)

White goes on to suggest a two-way account of therapy as being an approach that does not overstep ethical boundaries, but does 'transgress the oft-made work/life boundary distinction' (p. 132). This transgression requires us to recognize that we cannot meet and talk with people and hear the details of their lives, bear witness to their efforts to make changes in their lives, and not be touched emotionally and intellectually by this engagement. One way in which I have attempted to integrate this thinking into my practice is to think in terms of congruence, so that I am not required to shift political and philosophical positions radically across this work/life boundary.

Epston (2008) points out:

> You could almost palpably feel the relish with which Michael met the people who consulted him and how they in turn savoured those meetings.

It brought it home to me how enriching this work we do is to our lives – the 'two-way street' that Michael unashamedly so often spoke about. Michael always assumed that we were the lucky ones and I know he certainly considered himself to have always been the lucky one in such meetings. In fact, I think Michael looked up to those he met. (Epston, 2008, p. 4)

I certainly believe that we learn from the people we meet, and that what we learn has an impact on how we practise, how we think of other people in our practice, and how our own professional identity continues to develop.

Val, one of the women I met fairly early on in my career as a social worker, had requested services due to having experienced physical and emotional abuse numerous times from her husband. She told me that she read romance novels to learn how to behave properly so that her husband wouldn't beat her. She explained that her husband liked to call her his 'horny little angel' and so she read books in which the heroines could be described in these same terms so as to model her behaviours on theirs. Her comment ultimately led me to pursue my doctoral research in critical pedagogy and cultural studies, because I became concerned by how people in my practice were using popular cultural texts as a form of curriculum and learning. Shortly after beginning my doctoral programme, I heard Michael White for the first time at a narrative conversations conference (1995b). His comments about scaffolding learning and the recognition of the power of discourses within narrative practices brought my various interests together, and provided me with a beginning understanding of how I might be able to assist people in deconstructing such powerful messages as those within the romance discourse. Before I left the agency at which I worked when I met Val, I phoned her and told her what an impact she had had on my life and how she had inspired me in my further work. Val had a great influence on me in this two-way account of therapy.

Interestingly, one of the practitioners whom Hernández, Gangsei and Engstrom (2007) interviewed indicated that her experiences with a person who had died of cancer, and whose husband had been kidnapped, were so profound that she also committed to greater reflection and development of her therapy model, and planned to pursue further scholarly work. The practitioner reported:

She taught her children about finding and using their strengths and about coping with loss. I learned about how human beings have so many resources to face tragedy, the importance of spirituality, tolerance and the ability to survive. She left that message clearly to her sons and they survived well for eight months more until their father was released. She called me to the hospital the day she died and thanked me for teaching her how to die by talking with her about life. While everybody else spoke to her about death and dying, she said that I taught her and her children about life. (Therapist's words in Hernández, Gangsei & Engstrom, 2007, p. 236)

In one of the entry-level BSW courses that I teach, I use Saleebey's (2009) *The Strengths Perspective in Social Work Practice* to begin to encourage social work students to let go of mainstream problem-based discourses about what it means to help the people they will meet. Included in this fifth edition of the text is a chapter by Ed Canda on how a strengths perspective and spirituality can be integrated as an approach to managing the effects of chronic illness. He describes his own experiences living with cystic fibrosis. He also comments on his discomfort with the word resilience, because he worries that it suggests a return to a state prior to a crisis situation. He says that he thought about proposing the term prosilience, since it suggests moving forwards rather than backwards, but was worried that it would imply a movement along a developmental line. So he suggests transilience, which he describes as the process of leaping to a new, positive state of life. He goes on to say:

It encompasses coping, hoping, reacting, anticipating, preventing, promoting, and transcending. It is leaping beyond health and quality-of-life indicators. It is a life of transformation that is not restricted to social conventional ideas about health, illness, fitness, strength, goodness, ability, or disability. When a person addresses all of living and dying, including adversity, within a spiritual path of growth and transformation, then mundane and profound events can generate growth into expanded consciousness, more profound intimacy with the world, and liberation from the constraints of body bounded selfhood. (Canda in Saleeby, 2009, p. 89)

The account of the woman who learnt about life through dying and passed on her knowledge to her sons so that they could survive until their father was released by his kidnappers seems to be an example of something that could be described as transilience; it is difficult to imagine how we could not be affected both positively and with sadness by her situation. This example also reinforces Holloway's (2007) argument that professionals working in health and social services will need to develop a comfort level and the skills required for discussing issues of spirituality, especially when people are dying and are more apt to raise them.

Nonetheless, there is stress within work settings

Despite our commitments to working from a narrative perspective that privileges the insider knowledge of those people who consult us, to reflexivity and to consideration of the two-way account of therapy, all of which will contribute to vicarious resilience rather than vicarious trauma, we will still find ourselves at times working in stressful situations. Kearns and McArdle (2012), for instance, describe the significant budget constraints, negative representations of social work in the media, and at times having to work in defensive organizational cultures with risk-averse managerial approaches and rigid procedures, which can adversely affect social workers. How do we cope with these situations when we find ourselves in them?

Canda (in Saleebey, 2009) provides examples of how he manages stress, which he indicates is extremely important for him, as it is also necessary for managing the effects of his chronic illness. He has integrated various forms of mindfulness exercises and approaches influenced by both Eastern and Western philosophies, spirituality and religion. He uses guided relaxation and meditation and is committed to a healthy diet in a context of mindful eating. He describes how he visualizes the power and cleansing properties of water as he showers or takes his first sip of cool, clean water in the morning. He also mentions the importance of fun and humour, drumming, music and art, relationships with friends and family, and also developing his home with his wife so that it is peaceful and restorative. Finally, he points out the importance of nature in his spiritual practice.

I am inspired by Canda's reflections, but suggest that all his examples may not be of interest to everyone, and yet they may be of interest at different times in our lives. I have found that I have had to adjust my strategies as jobs, situations and interests have changed. Working in direct practice in a unionized agency-based setting meant rigid hours of work: 9–5 Mondays and Wednesdays and 9–9 Tuesdays and Thursdays. Although, as I have described earlier in this chapter, I was touched by the pain in people's stories and also positively affected and inspired, the rigidity of the work hours set up a boundary between work and home. There was also a general commitment by the majority of the other social workers in this office to take their hour-long lunch breaks. There was a kitchen available for our use and there were usually three or four people taking a lunch break at the same time so that we could eat together, chat, and perhaps even go on a walk to clear our heads from morning sessions, relax and rejuvenate for afternoon sessions. I also found the 40-minute drive home, out of the city and out into the suburbs through rolling hills, a good time to change focus and prepare myself for home life. Changing clothes as soon as I was home and not having access to work email at home triggered the shift and the separation of the two parts of life, which added a distance and comfort that I appreciated, and I think my family appreciated. Time with friends and family, gardening and making time for vacations all assisted with balance that supported self-care.

Work and life as an academic at a university are completely different from my early experiences in social services, but are probably not very different from many other practitioners' experiences of demands on their time these days. Now it is more difficult to separate work from the other parts of my life. Work is about reflecting, learning and teaching and, although class times are prescribed, the rest of my activities could go on at any time of the day or night. It is more difficult to judge the beginning and end of a work day and email is always accessible. People are able to email me at any time and most have come to expect fairly prompt replies. There is a much greater fluidity across any arbitrary boundary of day to evening or week to week-end. The opportunity to work from home is wonderful, and yet also adds to this sense of blurring of the various aspects of life.

A student recently mentioned her belief that social work is a calling; it is not just a job. I agree with her and think this is true of many of the helping professions. Bowles (in personal communication) has suggested that university careers are also often considered callings, and that the tension inherent in this is that people who feel called to certain careers run the risk of being taken advantage of as the calling takes over all aspects of their lives, administrators and managers expect more and more, and they lose all boundaries between work and home lives. On the other hand, I am not proposing setting up a dichotomy between work and home. As I have suggested earlier, I think that congruence between the various aspects of our lives assists with managing demands across those disparate aspects. It is useful, however, to be aware of strategies of self-care and the signs that perhaps we have begun to do too much for our careers and not focused as much on our families, friends and self.

I realize that I do not experience stress or burnout from working narratively with people, but I can feel fed up and overworked due to other demands of my job. During the first few years of my working as a newly qualified social worker, *The Joy of Stress* was published and promptly became a bestseller. I had a brief glance at it at the time, since I was curious about what so many people around me seemed to be reading. One observation in the book has remained with me: if your work involves lots of time with people, you might want to relax and deal with stress through time alone, whereas if your work is solitary you might benefit from time with people in order to manage stress. The simple idea is that balance can be helpful.

Patsiopoulos and Buchanan (2011) conducted a study in which they interviewed 15 counsellors regarding their practices of self-compassion and self-care, along with the resulting effects in their work lives. Three main themes emerged in their study: counsellors' stance in session; workplace relational ways of being; and finding balance through self-care strategies. In terms of 'stance in session', they discovered that self-compassion was practised in the following ways:

- Taking a stance of acceptance.
- Taking a stance of not knowing [*consistent with centring the insider knowledge of the person receiving services*].
- Compassionately attending to inner dialogue [*similar to my suggestions regarding the need for reflecting in action*].
- Being mindful of present experience [*see also Béres (2009) regarding the link between mindfulness and critical reflection*].
- Making time for self.
- Being genuine about one's fallibility. (Patsiopoulos & Buchanan, 2011, p. 303)

In relation to the second and third themes, they report that 'most participants referred to their self-care plans as a means of maintaining balance, which were described as holistic practices that contributed to their well-being and capacity for self-compassion in the workplace' (Patsiopoulos & Buchanan, 2011, p. 305). They indicate that one of the most common aspects of this type of self-care was making a commitment to leisure time. This leisure time included solitary time as well as time with friends and family. They go on to say:

Other strategies included getting enough sleep, eating nutritionally, exercising regularly, doing yoga, meditating, and getting massages. Some participants spoke about the importance of spending time in nature and engaging in creative projects like photography and painting. Others described helpful attitudes to life such as enjoying successes, allowing themselves to cry when they needed to, taking action as nonjudgmentally as possible, and using humor. Personal therapy, complementary healing practices, and spiritual/religious study and practices were also discussed. (Patsiopoulos and Buchanan, 2011, p. 305)

The more I spend time with others in counselling settings and in teaching, the more I have also become clearer about the benefits of solitary pursuits and time with my immediate family. I try to attend a silent weekend retreat at least once each year, but also appreciate time alone in my home and garden on a regular basis. The more I sit at a desk and write, sit and talk with people or stand while teaching, the more I need to make a commitment to activities that are more energetic so as again to aim for balance. I also enjoy losing myself in novels and movies and cannot imagine not having a dog as part of the family to remind me of the possibility of unbridled and unconditional joy.

Finally, as the notion of place has become of interest to me, I have come to realize how important are work settings and home, as physical places. Rothschild (2006), as she discusses structures of self-care, also provides practical suggestions for how to create a self-nurturing workplace. She suggests considering how things are arranged and what we are looking at while working. These ideas can initially seem to be more about decorating and meeting our own needs rather than others', but the physical space will have an impact on everyone who makes use of that space. Moffatt (1999) draws our attention to the manner in which Foucauldian notions of surveillance and control can be maintained through the structure and set-up of offices (pp. 224–5). It is possible and useful to reflect on the discourses and power relations that are created and reinforced due to the physical setting and arrangement of furniture; whether desks are set up to provide an outside view or positioned to create a divide between people is one simple example of how furniture arrangement may have an effect on self and other.

I have attempted to create a space in my work office that is both calming for myself and welcoming for others. I have also recently moved from one home to another in order to live in a community that encourages walking to shops and cafés and neighbourliness, and a home that provides views from most of the windows of trees and nature. I have found that sitting at the kitchen table watching the birds at the birdfeeders is a wonderful start to the day and something I would not have been remotely interested in, or appreciative of, 20 years ago. In fact, as I look for further methods of developing congruence between my professional and private lives, I am drawn more to the possibilities offered by simplicity and the practice of restraint (McFague, 2013; Merkel, 2003), which provide protection from the stress of the consumer-driven world that has impacts on all aspects of life and professional practice.

Finally, and also consistent with Rothschild's (2006) suggestions and Patsiopoulos and Buchanan's (2011) findings, I enjoy having groups of friends to visit so that I can cook for guests and extend hospitality. Although I might fret about cleaning and preparing meals as best I can, what makes it all worthwhile is nurturing friendships and being able to share the peace and relaxation that I am committed to developing in our home. Conversation and laughter certainly help a great deal when stressors of work could otherwise become all-consuming. Perhaps this has something to do with inserting a broader perspective and ensuring that I do not take myself too seriously.

A few examples of self-care

As it seemed important to finish this chapter, and in fact this book, with practical examples of how to engage in self-care, I thought that it would be useful to ask other narrative practitioners for their ideas. Meeting each month with a small group of like-minded narrative social workers in order to consult and support one another in our commitment to working narratively in a variety of practice settings is, in fact, one method of self-care, which assists in protecting us from day-to-day stressors in practice. Since my colleagues who meet in the consultation group are in direct practice, and most of them are in full-time practice within very challenging settings (i.e. child welfare, psychiatric healthcare, family health teams, violence against women team), it occurred to me that they would be the perfect group of practitioners with insider knowledge about issues of self-care to ask for practical examples. I thank them for their input.

Coralee Berlemont, BSW, MSW, RSW
(Social worker in In-patient Mental Health)

Case studies

Since learning about narrative practices I have discovered many of these techniques can also be used with oneself to build resilience, strength and the ability to continue on in the face of adversity. Like the individuals we work with, it is easy for any of us to get caught in webs of the problem storyline. Just like we would work with individuals curiously moving between the landscape of action and the landscape of identity, I have found we can open our own minds to new thoughts and feelings by viewing our own situations in similar ways. For example, remembering what I truly value has helped maintain hope and perseverance, renewing my strength and resilience in difficult times. Taking time to reflect on the areas within our lives we have neglected, forgotten, or even dismissed appears helpful in moving into alternative storylines about our own resilience, strength, courage and inner resources. Focusing on our problem storylines seems to dismiss aspects of ourselves: for example, instead of feeling courage, feeling weakness; instead of feeling strong, feeling worthless.

   I have also found it very helpful to find places where I feel relaxed with the ability to be in tune with my inner thoughts and feelings. This might consist of relaxing in a bath, taking a walk outside, scribbling thoughts and feelings into a journal, petting and cuddling with my pet in a quiet area or listening to music while sitting or lying in a relaxing position. Everyone has different ways of becoming in tune with their inner thoughts and feelings. Regardless of which approach is taken, I have found making time to not only reflect on my practices with individuals but also how I view myself can be invaluable. Learning narrative practices has helped me not give into the problem storyline but rather maintain hope during the many difficult situations we all face in life.

Joanna Bedggood, BSW, MSW, RSW (Director of Community Counselling and Violence against Women Services)
For me, an important part of my self-care strategy has been about noticing the messages I tell myself about the state of the world and about the work I do, and re-storying this if I need to. Some stories I have told myself through the years are: 'trauma makes the world go round', 'my counselling skills are inadequate' and 'outside of social services nobody cares about the rights of marginalized people or about issues related to poverty'.

Some of the ways I try to re-story the work in my head are: 'I am lucky to work in a sector with like-minded folks who care so much about these issues I care about. There are many others who care too – some who don't, but many who do', 'lots of things make the world go round … it's as complex as people themselves', 'better counselling can be done, but not by me – because I am doing my best and am always engaging in professional development, learning and reflection to increase the quality of my work'.

I also have been very interested lately in reading about the concept of 'vicarious resilience' and the idea of giving as much attention to the way the nature of our work enriches us personally as we do to the ways in which it impacts us negatively.

Diane Gingrich, BSW, MSW, RSW (Social worker, Intake Child Protection)
Self-care is a term that is often stressed in professional circles, but my experience would suggest that it is rarely actively encouraged by employers. Consequently, it has always been a struggle for my 'people pleasing' personality to recognize this requirement of the profession. However, these are a few things that I do to help me:

1. As a child protection worker, I am blessed to be surrounded by social workers each and every day. This allows me to be able to talk through the stories I have heard while meeting with individuals and families. Giving voice to the trauma and sadness we see on a daily basis is a key requirement to minimizing the possible impact of vicarious trauma. Dialogue and peer support have been priceless to me.

2. Being mindful of my internal dialogue, emotions and mental health, and not minimizing them, is important. It is critical that I recognize when I am feeling overwhelmed, and respond accordingly. Re-jigging my schedule, sometimes by sitting down with my supervisor to re-arrange my priorities (and to ensure that she understands what is currently on my plate); ensuring that I am getting enough sleep and eating well (because everything is bigger when you are not sleeping or feeling well); or taking a holiday are all useful responses. There have also been times in my life when I have had to walk away. This has been difficult, but I do not believe it to be an indicator of failure.

3. Self-care has to be *my* priority; no one else will take responsibility for this for me. There will always be someone competing for my time. Consequently, I have found scheduling my time around activities that I enjoy doing to be of great benefit, as it forces me to walk away and set some limits. These activities may be as mundane as taking responsibility for driving my kids to their programmes; a weekly scheduled coffee break with a friend; my daily walk; or time to watch my favourite television show/read my book, but these mundane activities provide balance.

4. Finally, I have to remind myself to give myself permission to make this a priority. Sometimes it feels that the weight of the world is on my shoulders and that if I don't respond immediately, the results will be devastating. Maybe this is true and maybe it is not, but this is not my sole responsibility to take on. We were not put in these positions to 'save the world', as much as we may feel otherwise. As a Christian woman, my faith is important to me and so I remember that even Jesus needed to take time for himself and walk away from healing and teaching in order to spend time on his own. Therefore, it is really okay for me to do the same and take time to spend time alone too.

Hiedi Britton-deJeu, BSW, MSW, RSW (Social worker with Family Health Team)

I believe that taking care of ourselves is critical to the work we do. I am reminded about the importance of self-care on a daily basis when I am talking with other people about the importance of their self-care.

First and foremost, I try to exercise (play on a sports team), eat balanced meals (when I can) and get 'good enough' rest. There is nothing like kicking a football to get out some stress and then laughing with your teammates when you miss the net. In fact, a sense of humour is also vital for managing stress.

I try to focus on positive or helpful views of situations, which often open up new opportunities and storylines for me that I would have missed otherwise. For example, I locked myself out of the house one day after a long day at work. I had to wait for my husband to arrive home and couldn't start supper. Thankfully, it was a beautiful day and I said to myself, 'Well, I guess, I was meant to be outside with the kids today,' and when I was able to make that shift in my thinking, I took advantage of the wonderful found time with my children.

I also use my faith for self-reflection and to pray for others when I feel an extra helping hand is needed. This helps me feel rooted and connected to a power bigger than myself, so I don't feel isolated in my efforts at helping others.

As a mum, I try to incorporate my 'self-care' activities with things that my kids also enjoy. For example, we all go to the YMCA together, listen to music and do arts and crafts. I love to do these activities and by doing them with my children, I decrease my feelings of 'mother's guilt', which can be toxic for a working mum. Although 'self-care' is about taking care of one's self, I also feel better when I know I'm taking care of my family and feel 'balanced', so finding ways to relax and do enjoyable things all together really helps with my personal self-care. Thankfully, I also have a very supportive husband who is truly my 'partner' and so I feel supported when I focus on my self-care.

When I do activities for myself, I am very protective of my free time and try to spend my time doing activities that help me develop new understandings or ways of looking at life. I enjoy reading novels or watching movies where society needs to be re-organized and heroes are developed that overcome oppression. I avoid activities that put me at risk of further vicarious trauma, such as reading stories with severe abuse or trauma. I also try to do activities where I don't have to think at all to give my brain a well-deserved break. I enjoy camping with my family and spending time immersed in nature. As soon as we pull up with our caravan, my brain turns off and I don't turn it back on until we leave the park.

Sandy Ferreira, BSW, MSW, RSW (Social Worker with youth in school settings, who has previously worked with men who had been charged with abuse of their partners)
I have frequently found myself bewildered by comments made by people when they learn of my career choice that suggest they could never be a social worker, since it must be so hard to listen to sad or traumatic stories all day. I have had difficulty responding to these comments in a way that reconciles my feelings because on the one hand, 'No, it isn't hard to listen to others,' and on the other hand, 'Yes, the stories we hear are difficult and do elicit a relational response in me.' However, ultimately, I believe that hearing an individual's story is not a burden but rather an honour and a privilege.

Being a part of the narrative consultation group and engaging in conversations with others who have a shared philosophy in our approach to practice, I have found myself reassured that the things we hear in people's stories cannot help but have an effect on us as well as on the teller of the story, and that this is okay.

I have found that working with a population that I enjoy can make a huge difference in stress levels and satisfaction. I remember at one point feeling uncertain about where my career was going, and what helped was realizing simply that I knew there was a specific group with whom I had always wanted to work. I currently work with this population and love what I do. My work fits with my hopes and in a lot of ways it doesn't feel like work. I can look back now and recognize that it was at times when I was feeling unsure about whether I was in the right place and with the right population that other stressors, such as a particular climate in an agency, crossed into my personal life.

Although I see myself as very fortunate in my role, engaging in a practice of self-care remains an important aspect of what I see as maintaining a good balance of the things that are important in my life. Complementing work commitments with spontaneity, and social time with family and friends, is always important. The activities themselves vary and can start on my commute as I'm listening, singing or laughing along to the radio. Trips to the gym, attending a yoga or fitness class, walking, coffee breaks and dinners or just quick visits with friends are all important to me. Sometimes even something as simple as reminding myself that there is always hope and maintaining a belief that things are bigger than me can make the difference.

Melissa Page Nichols, BSW, MSW, RSW (Social worker with a campus ministry team, who has previously worked with refugees and survivors of trauma)
In my work with people who experience oppression of a particularly encompassing nature that is exceedingly prevalent throughout the world, such as sexual violence towards women and girls, I have often encountered challenging moments: moments in which I am faced with an intense internal struggle of clashing values between my feminist, anti-oppressive narrative framework and the reality that is many women's lived experience. I believe that it is in the inter-connectedness of our humanity where we humbly encounter our own fragility and where we are sensitized to those who are made 'other'. It is in these moments that working from the de-centred narrative approach, where people are not to be 'fixed' or 'rescued', but to be assisted in coming to their own understandings about their experiences and accessing their own strengths in approaching the problems they are facing, certainly assists significantly in reducing emotional fatigue. I also greatly appreciate the assumption of hope and the belief in human capacity for change that I find to be inherent in the narrative commitment to moving away from totalizing accounts of people; a preferred way of being is possible, even for those labelled as 'personality disordered', 'addicted' or 'abuser'.

However, I have also come to understand, at least for myself, that there are two other critical components to my work: self-reflection and self-care. Along with self-reflection through clinical debriefing and consultation, I find myself drawn to both scheduled and spontaneous moments of self-reflection and self-care. The spontaneous moments might be taking myself to a coffee shop to enjoy a good book, taking a mindful walk around the block when I have a break between appointments, or going outside to enjoy my lunch on the park bench in front of a lovely courtyard garden at a church across the street from my office. The scheduled moments for me often take the form of a retreat day of silence, rest and journaling at the residence of the Sisters of St Joseph here in London, Ontario and monthly massage appointments. I am also eternally grateful to the incredible mentors, colleagues, friends and family who support me in my work and who help to keep me grounded.

Conclusion

I have focused a great deal in this book on the need to move away from totalizing or labelling accounts of people, and yet, as mentioned in the Preface, I continue to find that I think of myself as 'a narrative practitioner' despite the possibility, therefore, of totalizing myself as such. I continue describing myself as a narrative practitioner because I am committed to the underlying philosophy and politics of narrative therapy, and because I am excited by the methods of integrating these ideas into practice. I hope that I have managed to express my excitement about, and my belief in the value of, this approach to working with people. Since narrative practices continue to develop and evolve, I imagine that I will also continue to develop and change as a narrative practitioner.

I have attempted in this book as a whole, and this final chapter in particular, to present a clear description of the possibilities inherent in working as a narrative practitioner. I am pleased that colleagues have been willing to contribute experiences, reflections, case and documentation examples, as well as ideas about self-care. This has made the book richer, with a broader array of practice examples than I would have been able to provide if I had only been reflecting on my own practice. The fact that I have been able to include other people's reflections also represents another aspect of narrative therapy, which I greatly appreciate: many people and discourses are continually engaging with, and further shaping, the ongoing development and practice of narrative therapy. Narrative practices will not be stagnating, because narrative practitioners are committed to reflecting on the process and effects of their interactions with people and adjusting to feedback. This enables practitioners to respond to changing needs and to integrate developing areas of inquiry and knowledge.

The final themes in the second part of this book have been reiterated in this final chapter: critical reflection of practice and respect for diverse spiritual and faith traditions are crucial in order to engage ethically with people and be aware of resilience and vicarious resilience. I hope that narrative practitioners will continue to explore these areas further regarding their possible contributions in the health and social services.

Notes

1. Interestingly, he also points out that the ethics and regulation of the sexual act and conjugal arrangements developed in this period rather than within Christianity, when he says that it has too easily been attributed 'when it is not attributed to capitalism or "bourgeois morality"' (Foucault, 1994, p. 90).

2. One possible criticism of Foucault is his focus on Western, and of course male, philosophers. It would be fascinating, for another writing project, to examine the development of self-care in Indigenous and Eastern religions and philosophy.

Appendix 1

The following is the Narrative Individual Family Questionnaire (NIFQ) 1 as provided by Walter Bera of the Kenwood Therapy Center and discussed in chapter 5.

Name: _____ Date: _____

D.O.B. _____ Relationship to Family/Individual: _____

Narrative Individual Family Questionnaire 1 (NIFQ-1)

1. Who referred you or the family to the Kenwood Therapy Center?
   _____

2. What is the Problem or Situation that brought you to seek help at the Kenwood Center?
   _____
   _____

3. Names of the main person, or people, who are affected by the Problem and Why
   _____
   _____
   _____
   _____

Problems, Effects, People, Exceptions, Values and Meanings Evaluation

*Directions: Problems affect individuals, family members and concerned others in various ways. Please rate each item by circling the number indicating how difficult (or not) a Problem or Effect is for yourself (**Self**) and the person, or persons, you may be concerned (**Other**). Name the concerned Other person(s) and Why you gave the ratings. Use the back of the form if you need more room.*

1. Depression/Sadness?　　　　Self:　(Low) 1 2 3 4 5 6 7 8 9 10 (High)

　　　　　　　　　　　　　　Other:　(Low) 1 2 3 4 5 6 7 8 9 10 (High)

   Who/Why? _____
   _____
   _____

2. Suicide Risk/Self-Harm?   Self: (Low) 1 2 3 4 5 6 7 8 9 10 (High)

    Other: (Low) 1 2 3 4 5 6 7 8 9 10 (High)

    Who/Why? _____

    _____

    _____

3. Alcohol/Drug Abuse?   Self: (Low) 1 2 3 4 5 6 7 8 9 10 (High)

    Other: (Low) 1 2 3 4 5 6 7 8 9 10 (High)

    Who/Why? _____

    _____

    _____

4. Relationship Conflict?   Self: (Low) 1 2 3 4 5 6 7 8 9 10 (High)

    Other: (Low) 1 2 3 4 5 6 7 8 9 10 (High)

    Who/Why? _____

    _____

    _____

5. Anxiety/Worry?   Self: (Low) 1 2 3 4 5 6 7 8 9 10 (High)

    Other: (Low) 1 2 3 4 5 6 7 8 9 10 (High)

    Who/Why? _____

    _____

    _____

6. Verbal Abuse/Behavior?   Self: (Low) 1 2 3 4 5 6 7 8 9 10 (High)

    Other: (Low) 1 2 3 4 5 6 7 8 9 10 (High)

    Who/Why? _____

    _____

    _____

7. Sexual Abuse/Behavior?   Self: (Low) 1 2 3 4 5 6 7 8 9 10 (High)

    Other: (Low) 1 2 3 4 5 6 7 8 9 10 (High)

    Who/Why? _____

    _____

    _____

8. Physical Abuse/Behavior?   Self: (Low) 1 2 3 4 5 6 7 8 9 10 (High)

    Other: (Low) 1 2 3 4 5 6 7 8 9 10 (High)

    Who/Why? _____

    _____

    _____

9. Other Problem/Behavior?   Problem/Behavior Name: _____

    Self: (Low) 1 2 3 4 5 6 7 8 9 10 (High)

    Other: (Low) 1 2 3 4 5 6 7 8 9 10 (High)

Who/Why? _____

_____

_____

ASSESSMENT

Overall, why do you think there are these problems for yourself (**Self**) and the **Other** persons?

_____

_____

_____

_____

PROBLEM SOLVING

What is the <u>main</u> goal or hope you have for the first session?

_____

_____

What are your ideas on how that goal or hope can be accomplished?

_____

_____

_____

Why do you think you, and the other concerned people, want to change things <u>now</u>?

_____

_____

_____

Source: Bera, W. (2013)

Appendix 2

The following is the Narrative Individual Family Questionnaire (NIFQ) 2 as provided by Walter Bera of the Kenwood Therapy Center and discussed in chapter 5.

Name: _____ Date: _____

D.O.B. _____ Relationship to Family/Individual: _____

Narrative Individual Family Questionnaire 2 (NIFQ-2)

Updated: Problems, Effects, People, Exceptions, Values and Meanings Evaluation

Directions: We would like you to give us an update or progress summary on your view of the current individual and relationship therapy or consultation situation and your experience to date. For each item, name the concerned Other person(s) and Why you gave the rating. Your information and evaluation will be used to improve service to you and others. Use the back of the form if you need more room.

1. Depression/Sadness?

   Self: (Low) 1 2 3 4 5 6 7 8 9 10 (High)
   Other: (Low) 1 2 3 4 5 6 7 8 9 10 (High)

   Who/Why? _____
   _____
   _____

2. Suicide Risk/Self-Harm?

   Self: (Low) 1 2 3 4 5 6 7 8 9 10 (High)
   Other: (Low) 1 2 3 4 5 6 7 8 9 10 (High)

   Who/Why? _____
   _____
   _____

3. Alcohol/Drug Abuse?

   Self: (Low) 1 2 3 4 5 6 7 8 9 10 (High)
   Other: (Low) 1 2 3 4 5 6 7 8 9 10 (High)

   Who/Why? _____
   _____
   _____

4. Relationship Conflict? Self: (Low) 1 2 3 4 5 6 7 8 9 10 (High)
   Other: (Low) 1 2 3 4 5 6 7 8 9 10 (High)

   Who/Why? _____
   _____
   _____

5. Anxiety/Worry? Self: (Low) 1 2 3 4 5 6 7 8 9 10 (High)
   Other: (Low) 1 2 3 4 5 6 7 8 9 10 (High)

   Who/Why? _____
   _____
   _____

6. Verbal Abuse/Behavior? Self: (Low) 1 2 3 4 5 6 7 8 9 10 (High)
   Other: (Low) 1 2 3 4 5 6 7 8 9 10 (High)

   Who/Why? _____
   _____
   _____

7. Sexual Abuse/Behavior? Self: (Low) 1 2 3 4 5 6 7 8 9 10 (High)
   Other: (Low) 1 2 3 4 5 6 7 8 9 10 (High)

   Who/Why? _____
   _____
   _____

8. Physical Abuse/Behavior? Self: (Low) 1 2 3 4 5 6 7 8 9 10 (High)
   Other: (Low) 1 2 3 4 5 6 7 8 9 10 (High)

   Who/Why? _____
   _____
   _____

9. Other Problem/Behavior? Problem/Behavior Name: _____
   Self: (Low) 1 2 3 4 5 6 7 8 9 10 (High)
   Other: (Low) 1 2 3 4 5 6 7 8 9 10 (High)

   Who/Why? _____
   _____
   _____

EVALUATION OF ASSESSMENT/THERAPY/CONSULTATION EXPERIENCE

1. Overall Quality Rating? (Low) 1 2 3 4 5 6 7 8 9 10 (High)

2. What have you <u>liked most</u> about the assessment, therapy or consultation process?
   _____
   _____

3. What have you <u>liked least</u> about the assessment, therapy or consultation process?

    _____

    _____

4. What therapy/consultation, individual, relationship or other experience has been the <u>most helpful</u> for the problems and their effects?

    _____

    _____

5. What are your suggestions for how we could be <u>more helpful</u> in the future?

    _____

    _____

ASSESSMENT

Overall, <u>why</u> do you think there are these problems for yourself and the other persons?

_____

_____

_____

_____

PROBLEM SOLVING

What are the <u>main</u> goals or hopes you have for the current work?

_____

_____

What are <u>your</u> ideas on how those goals or hopes can be accomplished and <u>why</u> are they important to you and others?

_____

_____

_____

_____

Source: Bera, W. (2013)

Appendix 3

The following is the Informed Consent and Narrative Therapy Consultation Information sheet as provided by Walter Bera of the Kenwood Therapy Center and discussed in chapter 5.

Kenwood Center Informed Consent and Narrative Therapy and Consultation Information

The intention of this Kenwood Center information sheet is to help you and people, and the organizations and people you care about know some ideas and practices we, and people who have consulted us in the past, have found helpful. Our intention is to invite you and them into new and creative approaches to responding to the problems, issues or concerns that are to be addressed during consultations and projects.

Narrative Approaches

We use Narrative ideas and approaches as the foundation of our work at the Center. It can be called Collaborative Narrative Therapy, Collective Narrative Practice or Narrative Community Work depending on the context. They are a growing set of ethically based and innovative therapy ideas that recognize people use narrative, or story, to make meaning of their lives and identity and as such can re-author them. Such Narrative ideas and practices are becoming increasing widespread and accepted.

The consultant may ask you questions about your life and concerns to facilitate what we hope is a meaningful conversation of re-authoring life, family or community according to your intentions, purposes, values, beliefs, hopes, dreams, visions, and commitments to ways of living. We want to creatively consult some of the personal and professional stories, resources and ideas you may or may not have fully considered in the hope that they might provide new possibilities and ways to address the concerns that brought you here. And we invite you to creatively express yourself through writing, words, art, music, logic, etc. In addition, we are trained in and may suggest other possibly helpful, collaborative and research informed consultation approaches and ideas.

The Kenwood Center Team

You and your consultant have access to the knowledge and skills of our multidisciplinary team of licensed psychologists, marriage and family consultants, clinical social workers, alcohol and drug counselors, interns, outside people and professionals when needed, and our clinical and research library and bookstore of research, videotapes, audiotapes and DVDs. You can find out more by talking with your Kenwood consultant or visiting our website at www.kenwoodcenter.org.

Some Ideas and Practices That We Find Helpful in Our Work

Your Knowledge and Values Are Respected

We see people as knowledgeable in their own lives and view problems as separate from people. Narrative therapy assumes that people and communities have many skills, competencies, beliefs, values, commitments and abilities that will assist them to reduce the influence of problems in their lives.

The Person Is <u>Not</u> the Problem

We avoid thinking or speaking of those we consult with or their loved ones or community as the "Problem." Rather, the Problem is the Problem, and we strive, with compassion and understanding, to ally with people as they stand up to or change their relationship to problems and reclaim their lives, families and communities from their influence.

Externalized Conversation

As someone consulting here, you might notice that if you say, "I am depressed," your consultant might ask, "How did you notice Depression first influencing your life?" This is an example of how we separate the person from the problem. This can help move from what we call problem-saturated identities toward more rich and full descriptions of life and can help put problems in their broader contexts.

Life is Multi-storied

Just as one's preferred identity may be rendered invisible by problems, so also one may look back at life and see little, except a problem-saturated, hopeless history. Your consultant may ask unusual, exceptional, and curious questions that may help you put in words often thinly described, hidden stories of richer understanding, strength, possibility and hope. In this way, we find people can often creatively reclaim or construct, with the help/support of others, what we call preferred realities and identity.

Consultant: Influential, But De-centered

The consultant you talk with strives to be "influential but de-centered," working to keep central you and your ideas and preferences. We strive to be responsible collaborators and co-authors with those we work with, rather than pretending to be all-knowing experts to tell you how to live your life. While we may share some of our ideas, resources and experiences regarding some ways a problem can influence a life, based on what others have told us, we prefer to first acknowledge and build on your unique story, wisdom and resources. We view the consultant as skillful in respecting and making more visible your own preferred words, ideas, theories and practices of life, perhaps imposing some ill-fitting theoretical, cultural or societal mandates.

Collaborative: The Particular Context

We have found that problems can isolate us and make it hard to find options, possibilities and connections in our lives. As appropriate, we may ask you, with your full approval and understanding, to allow us to collaborate with key family members, relatives, friends, associates, and involved professionals, who may be helpful or concerned. Any requested assessment, report, or letter is reviewed with you. We strive to collaborate in sensitive, responsible, ethical, legal, diplomatic and creative ways.

The Background Context

The background of many problems can be a history or experience of injustice and cultural difficulty. We may spend some of our time considering such socially constructed, taken for granted stories of family, gender, culture, ethnicity, sexuality, economics, faith, etc., and their influences in your life and identity. This can help make such influences more visible and may help you decide more clearly if those ideas and practices may fit with what you want in your life and relationships.

Questions, Concerns, Complaints, Suggestions

Please feel free, at any time, to express any questions, concerns, or suggestions with your consultant, office staff or to Director Walter H. Bera, PhD at 612-377-9190 x 1. And please give us your thoughts on our work. We continue to develop from the suggestions and feedback of the many people and professionals we have worked with and, as such, continue to improve.

Signed Permission to Conduct Narrative Therapy, Consultation, Research, Evaluation and Follow-up

Your signature below confirms you have read this handout and give your legal consent to Narrative Therapy or Consultation and to complete brief therapy evaluations or allow videotaping to help inform our work and provide professional accountability, training, research and development. You also give us legal permission, to contact you by phone, email, text or other approved electronic media (e.g. Skype) or mail to check up on how things went or are going as part of our ongoing and follow-up care and research. You further agree to allow us to summarize or publish the results knowing that no personally identifying information will be disclosed. Please feel free to cross out any item or line you do not agree to and know it will have no impact on your therapy or consultation experience.

Signed: _____ Date: _____

Signed: _____ Date: _____

Signed: _____ Date: _____

Signed: _____ Date: _____

Signed: _____ Date: _____

Witness: _____ Date: _____

Source: Bera, W. (2013)

Appendix 4

This appendix contains the Individual–Family–Societal Narrative History, Evaluation and Assessment form as provided by Walter Bera of the Kenwood Therapy Center and described in chapter 5.

KENWOOD INDIVIDUAL–FAMILY–SOCIETAL NARRATIVE HISTORY, EVALUATION, ASSESSMENT, VALUES AND PLAN (RE-AUTHORING)

*(Complete in first 3–6 sessions using a **narrative question** format, in a collaborative manner, and respecting the person's preferred languaging and inviting their social/cultural/historical critiques for a rich narrative description)*

Person/"Client": _____ Interview Date(s): _____

Date of Birth: _____ Occupation/Spend time doing: _____

Gender ID: _____ Racial/Ethnic ID: _____ Interviewer(s): _____

Other descriptive information you would like to share?
_____
_____

What are the Problems, Concerns or Circumstances that bring you here?
_____
_____
_____
_____
_____

What are your Significant Family and other Relationships? *(Genogram to help visualize)*

Can you tell me the story of the Problems/Situations that bring you here? (In person's words/perspective) *Consider questions around 1. Externalized Histories of Problems (and Exceptions)? 2. Effects (in Relationship)? 3. Person's Evaluation? 4. Their Meaning/Assessment/Why? 5. Plans/Initiatives/Exceptions? 6. Anti-Problem/Problem Solving Team Members, Ideas, Practices, Skills, Knowledges, Learnings and Places? 7. Motivating and Precious: Values, Purposes, Intentions, Commitments, Beliefs, Hopes, Dreams and Visions of Life?*

_____

_____

_____

_____

_____

_____

_____

_____

_____

_____

_____

_____

_____

_____

_____

_____

_____

_____

_____

_____

_____

_____

_____

_____

_____

_____

_____

_____

_____

Education/Training History/Situation?

_____

_____

_____

Employment and Financial History/Situation?

_____

_____

_____

Religious/Spiritual/Philosophical History and Values?

_____

_____

_____

Significant legal, family or custody issues? Names/contact info we should have for a Collaborative ROI?

_____

_____

_____

Previous Therapy or Psychiatric History?

_____

_____

_____

Significant medical and medication/herbal use history? Assessment of current Physical Health Status?

_____

_____

_____

Name and Contact Info of health provider:

_____

_____

Permission for ROI? Yes? _____ No? _____

Name, relationship and contact information of persons we can contact in case of a Crisis or Emergency? *(Legally and ethically necessary because of our position and limitation as an outpatient therapy center. Two minimum.)*

1. _____

2. _____

3. _____

Alcohol and Drug History and Assessment.
Statement of Position Maps: 1. History. 2.Effects (in Relationship). 3. Evaluation. 4. Why or Meaning 5. Plan?

Alcohol:
_____
_____
_____
_____
_____

Marijuana:
_____
_____
_____
_____

Other Substances?:
Cocaine:
_____

Amphetamines:
_____

Depressants:
_____

Hallucinogens:
_____

Inhalants:
_____

Club Drugs:

Other?

Legal Prescription/Herbal Medication Use/History/Effects/Evaluation/Meaning

Pain Relievers:

ADHD meds:

SleepAids:

Others?

Nicotine:

Previous Chemical Health Treatment?

Other Common Concerns:
Statement of Position Maps: 1. History. 2.Effects (in Relationship). 3. Evaluation. 4. Why or Meaning 5. Plan?

Financial Health, Concerns or Spending issues?

Gambling History or Problems?

Internet/Computer/Social Media Use or Concerns?

_____
_____
_____

SUMMARY: What is your own, and others', assessment and meaning of your relationship to possibly mood altering substances, finances or compulsive behavior? Plans or initiatives for the future and why?

_____
_____
_____
_____
_____
_____
_____
_____
_____

Abuse and Neglect History/Assessment
Statement of Position Maps: 1. History. 2.Effects (in Relationship). 3. Evaluation. 4. Why or Meaning 5. Plan?

Sexual Abuse: Experiencing/Witnessing/Effects/Meaning/Initiatives?

_____
_____
_____
_____
_____

Physical Abuse: Experiencing/Witnessing/Effects/Meaning/Initiatives?

_____
_____
_____
_____
_____
_____

Emotional or Verbal Abuse: Experiencing/Witnessing/Effects/Meaning/Initiatives?

_____

_____

_____

_____

_____

_____

Neglect? Experiencing/Witnessing/Effects/Meaning/Initiatives?

_____

_____

_____

_____

_____

_____

Mental Status Exam and Safety Assessment:
Possible Effects of Depression/Grief/Sadness:

Appetite/Weight: Hopelessness:

_____   _____

Sleep: Interest in Activities:

_____   _____

Energy/Fatigue: Psychomotor Agitation/Lethargy
                                          (observed by self and others?):
_____

Self-Esteem:

_____   _____

Concentration/Indecisiveness: Worthlessness/Guilt:

_____   _____

Current Influence of Depression: (Low) 1 2 3 4 5 6 7 8 9 10 (High)

Any Suicide Attempts/Suicide Plans/Ideations/Methods (past and current):

_____

_____

Current Suicide Potential Scale: (Low) 1 2 3 4 5 6 7 8 9 10 (High)
Why?

_____

_____

If Current Suicide Concern: Motivation, method, opportunity? What is the prevention/intervention plan?

_____

_____

Any Fighting/Homicide Attempts/Plans/Ideations/Methods (past and current):

_____

_____

Current Homicide Potential Scale: (Low) 1 2 3 4 5 6 7 8 9 10 (High)
Why?

_____

_____

If Current Suicide/Homicide Concern: Motivation, method, opportunity? Describe prevention plan

_____

_____

_____

Possible Anxiety, Worry, Concerns? Effects, Meaning:

Significant anxieties and worries you have difficulty controlling?	Muscle Tension:
_____	Sleep
_____	_____
_____	Social:
_____	_____
Restless/On Edge:	Job:
Concentration/Mind Blank:	Family:
Irritable:	Panic Attacks:

Current Influence of Anxiety/Worry: (Low) 1 2 3 4 5 6 7 8 9 10 (High)

Possible Influence of "Thought Disorder" (disturbing thoughts, voices, dis-orientation, hallucinations, delusions)?

_____

Self-described General Appearance to Others:

_____

Mental Status Exam and Safety Summary Assessment and Meaning:
What is your own, and others' you know, current assessment of how you are doing personally and relationally? Why?

_____

_____

_____

_____

_____

_____

_____

RE-AUTHORING (MAP) LIVES AND RELATIONSHIPS SUMMARY

Why are you committed to changing your life and relationships now? What values, hopes, dreams and visions of life, that you hold precious, are motivating you? Can you tell me a story about these ideas and people that may have influenced you? (Use back of page if needed)

_____

_____

_____

_____

_____

_____

_____

Initiatives and Actions: Based on these above values, what are some of your initial plans, goals and initiatives?

1) _____

2) _____

3) _____

4) _____

5) _____

What Anti-problem skills, knowledges and places may be helpful in achieving these plans and goals for life?

1) _____

2) _____

3) _____

4) _____

5) _____

Anti-Problem Team: Who do you know or want to know who may be helpful in achieving these plans and goals?

1) _____

2) _____

3) _____

4) _____

5) _____

Any other thoughts or comments? How might other family members, relatives, friends, concerned professionals and the Kenwood Center, be helpful in these efforts?

_____

_____

_____

_____

_____

Preliminary DSM-IV Diagnosis: Signed Release and Consent for Assessment and Therapy Plan:

Axis I-Clinical Dx/Conditions:

_____

_____

Axis II-Personality Disorder/Developmental Disorder:

_____

_____

Axis III-General Medical Conditions:

_____

_____

Axis IV-Psychosocial/Environmental Stressors:

_____

_____

Axis V-Global Assessment of Functioning:

_____

0......10......20......30......40......50......60......70......80......90......100

Severe	Inability to	Serious	Moderate	Mild	Slight	Rare	No
Suicidal	Function in	Symp.	Symp.	Symp.	Trans	Symp.	Problems
Symp.	Most Areas				Functioning		
					Problems		

Signed: _____ Date: _____
                (Client/Person)

Signed: _____ Date: _____
                (Concerned Person)

Signed: _____ Date: _____
                (Concerned Person)

Signed: _____ Date: _____
      (Parent, Guardian or Legal Authority, if Client is
        Legally a Minor, Vulnerable or Mandated)

Signed: _____ Date: _____
      (Parent, Guardian or Legal Authority if a Client is
        Legally a Minor, Vulnerable or Mandated)

Signed: _____ Date: _____
                (Therapist or Intern)

Signed: _____ Date: _____
                (Therapist or Intern)

Signed: _____ Date: _____
                (Therapist or Intern)

Source: Kenwood Therapy Centre LLC (2013)

Appendix 5

This appendix contains a description of the narragram as provided by Walter Bera of the Kenwood Therapy Center and described in chapter 5.

Overview of the Narragram™: Upper Concept Map and Lower Timeline

Illustrated on the next page is the Narragram™: a visual of the narrative ideas and practices that are outlined in the previous *Kenwood Center Informed Consent and Narrative Therapy and Consultation Information* form. The Narragram™ consists of two interactive parts and assists in visualizing and capturing narrative therapy ideas and practices: the upper Concept Map and the lower Timeline. The overview of each part is from Berra, W. (2013). *Narragrams™: Visualizing Narrative Therapy* (2nd edn), Minneapolis, MN: Kenwood Center Publications, p. 25.

Narragram™ Concept Map

The Narragram™ Concept Map captures the names of the Problems, Effects, and their relationship (symbolized by the two arrows) to the Me, Myself and I domains as they emerge in the interview. They are placed into the major narrative conceptual categories (from right to left):

- **Problems:** The name or names for the situations or circumstances that cause difficulty and distress.
- **Effects:** The multiple effects of often multiple problems.
- **The Two Arrows (Dominant and Subordinate Plots):** The top arrow pointing at the Person represents how the problem affects the person (dominant plot). The lower arrow pointing at the Effects and Problems represents how the person affects the problem's effects (subordinate plot). These arrows also indicate the multiple Narrative question processes and ways of conceptualizing such as the process of evaluation of Effects, Double Listening, Dominant Plots/Subordinate Plots, and the various other narrative maps and question sequences. Of course, later we will get into much detail of the various maps and visual, musical and other approaches that can assist people to describe or share their experience of the problem's effects on them, and the ways they resist or counter the problem's influence.
- **Me:** The Person's anti-problem Places, People, Skills, and Knowledges used to resist or overcome the Effects of the Problems).
- **Myself:** Beliefs, Hopes, Dreams, Intentions, Values, Purposes, Visions of Life and Commitments that the person holds precious. This constitutes their non-structuralist identity.

- **I:** The observer or mindful self, which skillful narrative questioning evokes as people talk about the above.

Narragram™ Timeline

The Narragram™ Timeline is where one captures the person's stories in a sequence across time. This visualizes what Narrative practitioners call the Landscape of Action. At each point the interviewer can ask about the Effects of that particular Action in relationship to the Person and his or her life. The interviewer is reminded to ask the person's Evaluation of the effects and then the basis (or the Why) of that evaluation. What the person considers precious – Beliefs, Hopes, Dreams, Intentions, Values, Purposes, Visions of Life and Commitments – should underlie the Why of the person's evaluation. Michael White's Statement of Position Map 1 and 2 (White, 2007) as well as the concepts of his presentation of the tripartite "self" of Me, Myself and I (White, 2006) are the foundations of the Narragram™.

Narragram

Concept Map: Naming the Problems and Their Effects in Relationship to Me and Myself as I Observe Them

(Influenced by Grand Cultural-Historical "Normative' Narratives: Gender, Class, Ethnicity, Race, Sexuality, Religion, Theory, etc.)

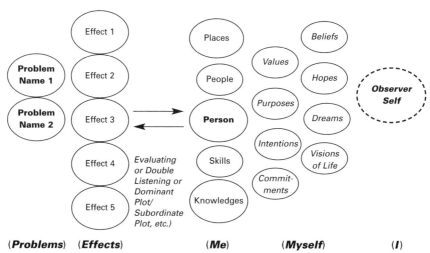

Timeline
Understanding and Living Our Lives Through Stories:
Events/People, Linked in Sequence, Across Time, According to Meaning or Plot
(Influenced by Grand Cultural-Historical "Normative" Narratives: Gender, Class, Ethnicity, Race, Sexuality, Religion, Theory, etc.)

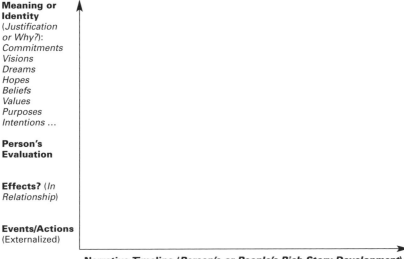

Meaning or Identity
(*Justification or Why?*):
Commitments
Visions
Dreams
Hopes
Beliefs
Values
Purposes
Intentions ...

Person's Evaluation

Effects? (*In Relationship*)

Events/Actions
(Externalized)

Narrative Timeline (*Person's or People's Rich Story Development*)

Source: Bera, W. (2013)

(Note: For a complete and updated set and detailed information on Collaborative Narrative Therapy Forms and Practices, including *Practicing Narrative Therapy in Modernist Settings: Innovative Approaches to Assessment, Diagnosis, Treatment Planning, Charting, and more* (Bera, 2014), please visit www.narrativebooks.com)

References

Aman, J. (2006). Therapist as host: Making my guests feel welcome, *International Journal of Narrative Therapy and Community Work*, 3, 3–10.

Aristarkhova, I. (2012). Hospitality and the maternal, *Hypatia*, 27(1), 163–81.

Barreto, A., & Grandesso, M. (2010). Community therapy: A participatory response to psychic misery, *International Journal of Narrative Therapy and Community Work*, 4, 33–41.

Bentley, J., & Paynter, N. (2011). *Around a Thin Place: An Iona Pilgrimage Guide*. Glasgow: Wild Goose Publications.

Bera, W. (2013a). *Practicing Narrative Therapy in Modernist Settings: Innovative Approaches to Assessment, Diagnosis, Treatment, Charting, and More*, Minneapolis, MN: Kenwood Center Publications.

Bera, W. (2013b). *Narragrams: Visualizing Narrative Therapy* (2nd edn), Minneapolis,MN: Kenwood Center Publications.

Béres, L. (1999). Beauty and the beast: The romanticization of abuse in popular culture, *European Journal of Cultural Studies*, 2(2), 191–207.

Béres, L. (2001). Romance, suffering and hope: Reflective practice with abused women. Unpublished doctoral dissertation. Toronto: University of Toronto.

Béres, L. (2002). Negotiating images: Popular culture, imagination, and hope in clinical social work practice, *Affilia: Journal of Women and Social Work*, 17(4), 429–47.

Béres, L. (2009). Mindfulness and reflexivity: The no-self as reflective practitioner. In S. Hick (ed.), *Mindfulness and Social Work: Reflective Practice and Interventions* (pp. 57–75), Chicago, IL: Lyceum Books.

Béres, L. (2010). Narrative therapy ideas and practices for working with addictions. In R. Csiernik & W.S. Rowe (eds), *Responding to the Oppression of Addiction: Canadian Social Work Perspectives*, 2nd edn (pp. 88–102), Toronto: Canadian Scholars Press.

Béres, L. (2012). A thin place: Narratives of space and place, Celtic spirituality and meaning, *Journal of Religion and Spirituality in Social Work: Social Thought*, 31(4), 394–413.

Béres, L. (2013). Celtic spirituality and postmodern geography: Narratives of engagement with place, *Journal for the Study of Spirituality*, 2(2), 170–85.

Béres, L., & Page Nichols, M. (2010). Narrative therapy group interventions with menwho have used abusive behaviors: Are they any different? *Families in Society: The Journal of Contemporary Social Services*, 91(1), 60–66.

Béres, L., Bowles, K., & Fook, J. (2011). Narrative therapy and critical reflection on practice: A conversation with Jan Fook, *Journal of Systemic Therapies*, 30(2), 81–97.

Béres, L., Bartholemew, A., Braaksma, H., Cowling, J., LaRochelle, N., & Taylor, A. (2008). The professor as 'not-knowing': Unsettling the expected in social work education, *Radical Pedagogy*, 9(20).

Berry, T. (1988). *The Dream of the Earth*. San Francisco, CA: Sierra Club Books.

Besthorn, F. H. (2012). Deep ecology's contributions to social work: A ten year retrospective, *International Journal of Social Welfare*, 21(3), 248–59.

Bird, J. (2008). *Talk That Sings: Therapy in a New Linguistic Key*. Auckland: Edge Press.

Bracken, P. (2012) Post psychiatry – Reaching beyond the technological paradigm in mental health. Lecture presented to the Forum for Existential Psychology and Therapy at the University of Copenhagen, available at http://www.youtube.com/watch?v=cV5RKT6Q8qU, accessed 16 December 2013.

Bradley, I. (2009). *Pilgrimage: A Spiritual and Cultural Journey*. Oxford: Lion Hudson.

Bradley, I. (2010). *The Celtic Way*. London: Darton, Longman and Todd.

Brookfield, S. D. (1995). *Becoming a Critically Reflective Teacher*. San Francisco, CA: Jossey-Bass.

Canda, E. R. (1988). Spirituality, diversity, and social work practice, *Social Casework*, 69(4), 238–47.

Canda, E. R. (2009) Chronic illness and transilience along my spiritual path. In D. Saleebey (ed.), *The Strengths Perspective in Social Work Practice*, 5th edn (pp. 72–90), Boston, MA: Pearson Education.

Carey, M., Walther, S., & Russell, S. (2009). The absent but implicit: A map to support-therapeutic enquiry, *Family Process*, 48(3), 319–31.

Chambon, A. S. (1999). Foucault's approach: Making the familiar visible. In A.S. Chambon, A. Irving & L. Epstein (eds), *Reading Foucault for Social Work* (pp. 51–81), New York: Columbia University Press.

Chang, J. (2010). Hermeneutic inquiry: A research approach for postmodern therapists, *Journal of Systemic Therapies*, 29(1), 19–32.

Charon, R. (2006). *Narrative Medicine: Honoring Stories of Illness*, Oxford: Oxford University Press.

Chittister, J. (2004[1994]). *The Rule of Benedict: Insights for the Ages*. New York: Crossroads Publishing.

Coates, J. (2007). From ecology to spirituality and social justice. In J. Coates, J. R. Graham & B. Swartzentruber, with B. Ouellette (eds), *Spirituality and Social Work: Selected Canadian Readings* (pp. 213–28), Toronto: Canadian Scholars Press.

Coates, J., & Besthorn, F. H. (2010). Building bridges and crossing boundaries: Dialogues in professional helping, *Critical Social Work*, 11(3), 2–7, available at http://www.uwindsor.ca/criticalsocialworker/2010-volume-11-no.3, accessed 16 March 2013.

Cook, C., Powell, A., & Sims, A. (eds) (2009). *Spirituality and Psychiatry*, Glasgow: RCPsych Publications.

Cooper, S. (2011). Narrative community practice: Neighboring communities revisited, *Journal of Systemic Therapies*, 30(3), 12–25.

Crisp, B. (2010). *Spirituality and Social Work*, Farnham: Ashgate.

D'Cruz, H., Gillingham, P., & Melendez, S. (2007). Reflexivity, its meanings and relevance for social work: A critical review of the literature, *British Journal of Social Work*, 37, 73–90.

Davies, O., & O'Loughlin, T. (1999). *Celtic Spirituality*, New York: Paulist Press.

Deleuze, G., & Parnet, C. (2002). *Dialogue II*, London: Continuum.

Denborough, D. (2008). *Collective Narrative Practice: Responding to Individuals, Groups and Communities Who Have Experienced Trauma*, Adelaide: Dulwich Centre Publications.

Denborough, D., Freedman, J., & White, C. (2008). *Strengthening Resistance: The Use of Narrative Practices in Working with Genocide Survivors*, Adelaide: Dulwich Centre Publications.

Derrida, J. (1974). *Of Grammatology* (G. Chakravorty, trans.), Baltimore, MD: John Hopkins University Press.

Dooley, M., & Kavanagh, L. (2007). *The Philosophy of Derrida*, Montreal: McGill-Queens University Press.

Duvall, J., & Béres, L. (2011). *Innovations in Narrative Therapy: Connecting Practice, Training, and Research*, New York: W.W. Norton.

Duvall, J., & Young, K. (2009). Keeping faith: A conversation with Michael White, *Journal of Systemic Therapies*, 28(1), 1–18.

Ellison, R., Rhodes, P., Madden, S., Miskovic, J., Wallis, A., Baille, A., Kohn, M., & Touyz, S. (2012). Do the components of manualized family-based treatment for anorexia nervosa predict weight gain? *International Journal of Eating Disorders*, 45(4), 609–14.

Epston, D. (2008). Saying hullo again: Remembering Michael White, *Journal of Systemic Therapies*, 27(3), 1–15.

Epston, D. (2009, May 4–8). *Five Day Intensive with David Epston*. Sponsored by Brief Therapy Training-International (a division of Hincks-Dellcrest Centre, Gail Appel Institute), Toronto, Canada.

Epston, D. (2012, October 9–11). *Master Class*. Sponsored by Re-authoring Teaching: Creating a Collaboratory, Waltham, VT, USA.

Falicov, C. J. (2007). Working with transnational immigrants: Expanding meanings of family, community, and culture, *Family Process*, 46(2), 157–71.

Ferguson, H. (2003). Outline of a critical best practice perspective on social work and social care, *British Journal of Social Work*, 33, 1005–24.

Fisher, A. (2005). Romance and violence: Practices of visual map making and documentation in conversations about men's abuse to women. *Catching the Winds of Change: Conference Proceedings* (pp. 115–23). Toronto: Brief Therapy Network.

Fisher, A., & Augusta-Scott, T. (2003, May 28). *Innovations in Practice: Working with Men Who Abuse*. Workshop at the Brief Therapy Network 2nd Annual Conference: Theory, Practice, and Practicality. Sponsored by Brief Therapy Training International (a division of Hincks-Dellcrest Centre, Gail Appel Institue), Toronto, Canada.

Fook, J. (1999). Critical reflectivity in education and practice. In B. Pease & J. Fook (eds), *Transforming Social Work Practice: Postmodern Critical Perspectives* (pp. 195–208), St. Leonards, Australia: Allen and Unwin.

Fook, J. (2000). Deconstructing and reconstructing professional expertise. In B. Fawcett, B. Featherstone, J. Fook & A. Rossiter (eds), *Practice and Research in Social Work: Postmodern Feminist Perspectives* (pp. 104–19), London: Routledge.

Fook, J. (2002). Theorizing from practice: Towards an inclusive approach to social work research, *Qualitative Social Work*, 1(1), 79–95.

Fook, J. (2003). Critical social work: The current issues, *Qualitative Social Work*, 2(2), 123–30.

Fook, J., & Gardner, F. (2007). *Practising Critical Reflection: A Resource Handbook*, Maidenhead: Open University Press/McGraw-Hill.

Foucault, M. (1965) *Madness and Civilization: A History of Insanity in the Age of Reason*. New York: Random House.

Foucault, M. (1994). *Ethics: Subjectivity and Truth* (P. Rabinow, ed., R. Hurley & others, trans), New York: New Press.

Freire, P. (1970). *Pedagogy of the Oppressed* (M. Bergman Ramos, trans.), New York: Seabury Press.

Furlong, M. (2008). The multiple relationships between the discipline of social work and the contributions of Michael White, *Australian Social Work*, 61(4), 403–20.

Geertz, C. (1973). *The Interpretation of Cultures: Selected Essays.* New York: Basic Books.

Gilbert, T. (2009). Ethics in social work: A comparison of the international statement of principles in social work with the code of ethics for British social workers, *Journal of Social Work Values and Ethics*, 6(2).

Giroux, H. A., & Simon, R. I., with contributors (1989). *Popular Culture, Schooling, and Everyday Life*, Granby, MA: Bergin and Garvey.

Goffman, E. (1961). *Asylums: Essays in the Social Construction of Mental Patients and Other Inmates*, New York: Doubleday.

Harrison, G., & Melville, R. (2010). *Rethinking Social Work in a Global World*, Basingstoke: Palgrave Macmillan.

Hernández, P., Gansei, D., & Engstrom, D. (2007). Vicarious resilience: A new concept in work with those who survive trauma, *Family Process*, 26(2), 229–41.

Hibel, J., & Polanco, M. (2010). Tuning the ear: Listening in narrative therapy, *Journal of Systemic Therapies*, 29(1), 51–66.

Holloway, M. (2007). Spiritual need and the core business of social work, *British Journal of Social Work*, 37(2), 265–80.

Holloway, M., & Moss, B. (2010). *Spirituality and Social Work*, Basingstoke: Palgrave Macmillan.

hooks, b., (1994). *Outlaw Culture: Resisting Representation*, New York: Routledge.

Hurley, D. J., Martin, L., & Hallberg, R. (2013). Resilience in child welfare: A social work perspective, *International Journal of Child, Youth, and Family Studies*, 4(2), 259–73.

Irving, A. (2006). Being is not syntactical: Ethics as intensities, *Canadian Social Work Review*, 23(1/2), 131–7.

Jenkins, A. (1990). *Invitations to Responsibility: The Therapeutic Engagement of Men Who Are Violent and Abusive*, Adelaide: Dulwich Centre Publications.

Kearns, S., & McArdle, K. (2012). 'Doing it right?' – accessing the narratives of identity of newly qualified social workers through the lens of resilience: 'I am, I have, I can', *Child and Family Social Work*, 17, 385–94.

Lassiter, L. E. (2005). *The Chicago Guide to Collaborative Ethnography*, Chicago, IL: University of Chicago Press.

Lysack, M. (2010). Environmental decline, loss, and biophilia: Fostering commitment in environmental citizenship, *Critical Social Work*, 11(3), 48–66, available at http://www.uwindsor.ca/criticalsocialworker/2010-volume-11-no.3, accessed 16 March 2013.

MacArthur, E. M. (2007). *Columba's Island: Iona from Past to Present*, Edinburgh: Edinburgh University Press.

Madigan, S. (2011). *Narrative Therapy*, Washington, DC: American Psychological Association.

Maisel, R., Epston, D., & Borden, A. (2004). *Biting the Hand That Starves You: InspiringResistance to Anorexia/Bulimia*, New York: W.W. Norton.

McFague, S. (2013). *Blessed Are the Consumers: Climate Change and the Practice of Restraint*, Minneapolis, MN: Fortress Press.

Merkel, J. (2003). *Radical Simplicity: Small Footprints on a Finite Earth*, Gabriola, BC: New Society.

Moffatt, K. (1999). Surveillance and government of the welfare recipient. In A. S. Chambon, A. Irving, & L. Epstein (eds), *Reading Foucault for Social Work* (pp. 219–46), New York: Columbia University Press.

Mullaly, B. (2006). Forward to the past: The 2005 CASW code of ethics, *Canadian Social Work Review*, 23(1/2), 145–50.

Munro, E. (2011). *The Munro Review of Child Protection: Final Report: A Child-Centred System*, available at *www.education.gov.uk/munroreview*, accessed 7 August 2012.

Myerhoff, B. (1982). Life history among the elderly: Performance, visibility and remembering. In J. Ruby (ed.), *A Crack in the Mirror: Reflexive Perspectives in Anthropology*, Philadelphia: University of Pennsylvania Press.

Myerhoff, B. (1986). Life not death in Venice: Its second life. In V. Turner & E. Bruner (eds), *The Anthropology of Experience*, Chicago: University of Illinois Press.

Myerhoff, B. (2007). *Number Our Days.* (Produced and directed by L. Littman). Santa Monica, CA: Direct Cinema.

O'Loghlin, T. (2000). *Celtic Theology: Humanity, World and God in Early Irish Writings*, London: Continuum.

Parton, N. (2003). Re-thinking *professional* practice: The contributions of social constructionism and the feminist 'ethics of care,' *British Journal of Social Work*, 33(1), 1–16.

Patsiopoulos, A. T., & Buchanan, M. J. (2011). The practice of self-compassion in counseling: A narrative inquiry, *Professional Psychology: Research and Practice*, 42(4), 301–7.

Payne, M. (2006). *Narrative Therapy: An Introduction for Counselors*, 2nd edn, London: Sage.

Payne, M., & Askeland, G. A. (2008). *Globalization and International Social Work: Postmodern Change and Challenge*, Aldershot: Ashgate.

Pentecost, M., & Speedy, J. (2006, March 2). Poetic mindedness and poetic writing: A means of 'double listening' towards, and capturing, the stories people tell in therapeutic conversations, International Narrative Therapy Festive Conference, Adelaide, Australia.

Rossiter, A. (2006). The 'beyond' of ethics in social work, *Canadian Social Work Review*, 23(1/2), 139–44.

Rothschild, B. (2006). *Help for the Helper: The Psychophysiology of Compassion Fatigue and Vicarious Trauma*, New York: W.W. Norton.

Ruch, G., Turney, D., & Ward, A. (2010). *Relationship-Based Social Work*, London: Jessica Kingsley.

Russell, S., & Carey, M. (2004). *Narrative Therapy: Responding to Your Questions*, Adelaide: Dulwich Centre Publications.

Russell, S., Markey, C., Denborough, D., & White, C. (2006). *Seven Month Narrative Therapy Training Programme*, Adelaide: Dulwich Centre Publications.

Saleebey, D. (2009). *The Strengths Perspective in Social Work Practice*, 5th edn, Boston, MA: Pearson Education.

Scharper, S. B. (2013). *For Earth's Sake: Towards a Compassionate Ecology*, Toronto: Novalis.

Schön, D. A. (1983). *The Reflective Practitioner: How Professionals Think in Action*, New York: Basic Books.

Speedy, J. (2005). Using poetic documents: An exploration of poststructuralist ideas and poetic practices in narrative therapy, *British Journal of Guidance & Counselling*, 33(3), 283–98.

Toukmanian, S. G., & Rennie, D. L. (eds) (1992). *Psychotherapy Process Research: Paradigmatic and Narrative Approaches*, London: Sage.

Tuhiwai Smith, L. (1999). *Decolonizing Methodologies: Research and Indigenous Peoples*, London: Zed Books.

Turner, V. (1986). Dewey, Dilthey, and drama: An essay in the anthropology of experience. In V. Turner & E. Bruner (eds), *The Anthropology of Experience*, Chicago, IL: University of Illinois Press.

van Gennep, A. (1960). *The Rites of Passage*, Chicago, IL: University of Chicago Press. (Original work published in 1909.)

Waldegrave, C., Tamasese, K., Tuhanka, F., & Campbell, W. (2003). *Just Therapy – A Journey: A Collection of Papers from the Just Therapy Team, New Zealand*, Adelaide: Dulwich Centre Publications.

White, C., & Denborough, D. (2005). *A Community of Ideas: Behind the Scenes*, Adelaide: Dulwich Centre Publications.

White, M. (1988, Spring). Saying hullo again: The incorporation of the lost relatioship in the resolution of grief. *Dulwich Centre Newsletter*, 7–11.

White, M. (1994). *Recent Developments in the Narrative Approach*, American Association of Marriage and Family Therapy (AAMFT): Learning Edge Series videotape of 50th anniversary conference in Miami Beach, Florida.

White, M. (1995a). *Re-authoring Lives: Interviews and Essays*, Adelaide: Dulwich Centre Publications.

White, M. (1995b, March 22 & 23). Therapeutic conversations as collaborative inquiry. Two-day training sponsored by the Brief Therapy Training Centres International (a division of Hincks-Dellcrest Centre, Gail Appel Institute), Toronto, Canada.

White, M. (1997). *Narratives of Therapists' Lives*, Adelaide: Dulwich Centre Publications.

White, M. (2000). *Reflections on Narrative Practices: Essays and Interviews*, Adelaide: Dulwich Centre Publications.

White, M. (2004). *Narrative Practice and Exotic Lives: Resurrecting Diversity in Everyday Life*, Adelaide: Dulwich Centre Publications.

White, M. (2005, April 11 & 12). *Mapping Narrative Conversations*. Two-day training, sponsored by Brief Therapy Training Centres International (a division of Hincks-Dellcrest, Gail Appel Institute), Toronto, Canada.

White, M. (2006, March 3). *Addressing the Consequences of Trauma*. International Narrative Therapy Festive Conference, Adelaide, Australia.

White, M. (2007a). *Maps of Narrative Practice*, New York. W.W. Norton.

White, M. (2007b, December 10–15). *Level 2 Narrative Therapy Training*. Sponsored by the Dulwich Centre, Adelaide, Australia.

White, M., & Epston, D. (1990). *Narrative Means to Therapeutic Ends*. New York: W.W. Norton.

Wilson, S. (2008). *Research Is Ceremony: Indigenous Research Methods*, Halifax: Fernwood Publishing.

Wyschogrod, E. (1989). Derrida, Levinas, and violence. In H. J. Silverman (ed.), *Continental Philosophy II: Derrida and Deconstruction* (pp. 182–200), New York: Routledge.

Zapf, M. K. (2007). Profound connections between person and place: Exploring location, spirituality, and social work. In J. Coates, J. R. Graham, & B. Swartzentruber, with B. Ouellette (eds), *Spirituality and Social Work: Selected Canadian Readings* (pp. 229–42), Toronto: Canadian Scholars Press.

Zapf, M. K. (2010). Social work and the environment: Understanding people and place, *Critical Social Work*, 11(3), 30–46, available at http://www.uwindsor.ca/criticalsocialworker/2010-volume-11-no.3, accessed 16 March 2013.

Index

Note: Page references in **bold** indicate a figure on that page.